THE GHOST

OF

RICHARD THE THIRD.

A POEM,

PRINTED IN 1614, AND

FOUNDED UPON SHAKESPEARE'S HISTORICAL PLAY.

REPRINTED FROM THE ONLY KNOWN COPY

IN THE BODLEIAN LIBRARY.

WITH AN INTRODUCTION AND NOTES

BY

J. PAYNE COLLIER, ESQ.

LONDON:

PRINTED FOR THE SHAKESPEARE SOCIETY.

1844.

Printing Statement:

Due to the very old age and scarcity of this book, many of the pages may be hard to read due to the blurring of the original text, possible missing pages, missing text, dark backgrounds and other issues beyond our control.

Because this is such an important and rare work, we believe it is best to reproduce this book regardless of its original condition.

Thank you for your understanding.

COUNCIL

OF

THE SHAKESPEARE SOCIETY.

President.

THE MOST NOBLE THE MARQUESS OF CONYNGHAM.

Vice-Presidents.

RT. HON. LORD BRAYBROOKE, F.S.A.

RT. HON. LORD FRANCIS EGERTON, M.P.

RT. HON. THE EARL OF GLENGALL.

RT. HON. EARL HOWE.

RT. HON. LORD LEIGH.

RT. HON. THE EARL OF POWIS.

AMYOT, THOMAS, ESQ., F.R.S., TREAS. S.A.

AYRTON, WILLIAM, ESQ., F.R.S., F.S.A.

BOTFIELD, BERIAH, ESQ., M.P., F.R.S., F.S.A.

BRUCE, JOHN, ESQ., F.S.A.

CLERKE, MAJOR T. H. SHADWELL, K.H., F.R.S.

COLLIER, J. PAYNE, ESQ., F.S.A., DIRECTOR.

COOPER, C. PURTON, ESQ., Q.C., F.R.S., F.S.A.

CORNEY, BOLTON, ESQ.

CUNNINGHAM, PETER, ESQ., TREASURER.

DICKENS, CHARLES, ESQ.

DYCE, REV. ALEXANDER.

FIELD, BARRON, ESQ.

HALLAM, HENRY, ESQ., F.R.S., V.P.S.A.

HALLIWELL, J. O., ESQ., F.R.S., F.S.A.

PETTIGREW, T. J., ESQ., F.R.S. F.S.A.

PLANCHÉ, J. R., ESQ., F.S.A.

SHARPE, THE REV. LANCELOT, M.A., F.S.A.

THOMS, WILLIAM J., ESQ., F.S.A.

TOMLINS, F. GUEST, ESQ., SECRETARY.

WATSON, SIR FREDERICK BEILBY, K.C.

WRIGHT, THOMAS, ESQ., M.A., F.S.A.

INTRODUCTION.

The ensuing poem, which is intimately connected in matter and manner with Shakespeare's "Richard the Third," and which would probably not have been written but for the extreme popularity of that historical tragedy, has been noticed and quoted, for the first time, in the "Life" of our great dramatist, prefixed to the recent impression of his works, published by Messrs. Whittaker and Co. Our reprint is made from the sole existing copy, preserved in the Bodleian Library, and unknown to the previous editors of Shakespeare, as well as to all bibliographical antiquaries.

The poem is divided into three parts—the "Character," the "Legend," and the "Tragedy" of Richard the Third; and the following obvious and highly laudatory allusion to Shakespeare commences the second portion of the work :—

> " To him that impt my fame with Clio's quill
> Whose magick rais'd me from oblivion's den,
> That writ my storie on the Muses' hill,
> And with my actions dignifi'd his pen ;
> He that from Helicon sends many a rill,
> Whose nectared veines are drunke by thirstie men ;
> Crown'd be his stile with fame, his head with bayes,
> And none detract, but gratulate his praise.

Yet if his scænes have not engrost all grace
　　The much fam'd action could extend on stage;
If time or memory have left a place
　　For me to fill, t' enforme this ignorant age,
To that intent I shew my horrid face,
　　Imprest with feare, and characters of rage:
　　　　Nor wits, nor chronicles, could ere containe
　　　　The hell-deepe reaches of my soundlesse braine."

The author professes on his title-page to relate "more" regarding Richard the Third than was contained "in Chronicles, Plays, or Poems;" but it will be clear to those who read the following pages that to no previous writer has he been so much indebted as to Shakespeare. The incidents, or most of them, are of course matters of history; but in the treatment of them, and in much of the phraseology of his poem, the author has mainly copied our great dramatist, and a few of the more striking resemblances are pointed out in the notes. The writer has, in fact, done with respect to " Richard the Third," in verse, very much what was done with respect to " Pericles " in prose : a narrative is constructed out of a drama, the writer availing himself of the popularity of the subject in order to attract public attention and interest. It is the only specimen of the kind, and of that date, in our language with which we are acquainted ; for, although poems derived from history are sufficiently numerous, we know of none confessedly founded, as it were, upon a play : in this instance it has the additional recommendation of being founded upon a play by Shakespeare.

The form chosen by the author is that in which the legends in " The Mirror for Magistrates " are written,

where the ghost of the person is supposed to re-
late his own history. Niccols published his " Winter
Night's Vision," as a sequel to " The Mirror for Magis-
trates," in 1610; and there, as most persons are aware,
is found " The lamentable Lives and Deaths of the
two young Princes, Edward the Fifth and his brother
Richard, Duke of York," as well as " The tragical
Life and Death of King Richard the Third." It may
be considered remarkable that, although Shakespeare's
" Richard the Third," in 1610, had probably been on
the stage for sixteen or seventeen years, and had gone
through at least four editions, Niccols makes so little
use of it, and has not the most remote allusion to it:
only in one passage can we trace any direct likeness,
and there it is by no means close, as may be seen by
the subjoined quotation. Richard is speaking of the
time after he had killed Henry VI. in the Tower:—

> " He dead, the battels fought in field before
>   Were turn'd to meetings of sweet amitie;
> The war-gods thundring cannons dreadful rore,
>   And ratling drum-sounds warlike harmonie,
>   To sweet tun'd noise of pleasing minstralsie;
> The haile-like shot to tennis balls were turn'd,
> And sweet perfumes in stead of smoakes were burn'd.
>
> God Mars laid by his launce and tooke his lute,
>   And turn'd his rugged frownes to smiling lookes;
> In stead of crimson fields, wars fatall fruit,
>   He bath'd his limbes in Cypris warbling brookes,
>   And set his thoughts upon her wanton lookes:
> All noise of war was husht upon our coast;
> Plentie each where in easefull pride did boast."—p. 753.

Steevens, referring to the preceding stanzas, says that
"*more probably* Niccols was indebted to Shakespeare
than Shakespeare to him:" it would have puzzled
Steevens to show how it was *possible* for Shake-
speare to have been indebted to an author who pub-
lished his work thirteen years after "Richard the
Third" came from the press. John Lyly has this pas-
sage in his play, "Alexander and Campaspe," 4to, 1584,
but the resemblance is so trifling and distant, that we
do not think Shakespeare had it even in his mind when
he wrote Gloucester's soliloquy: it appeared, however,
just as many years before "Richard the Third" was
printed as Niccols's poem did after it:—"Is the warlike
sound of drum and trump turned to the soft noise of
lyre and lute? the neighing of barbed steeds, whose
loudness filled the air with terror, and whose breaths
dimmed the sun with smoke, converted to delicate
tunes and amorous glances?"

It will be observed that our quotation from Niccols's
"Winter Night's Vision" is in the ancient English form
of stanza employed by Chaucer, Lydgate, and other
early poets; while the author of "The Ghost of Richard
the Third" employs the Italian *ottava rima*, which may,
or may not, be considered an improvement. We do not
discover any connexion between the two poems, except-
ing those inevitable coincidences which arise out of the
fact, that both poets employed the same historical inci-
dents. The author of "The Ghost of Richard the
Third" seems almost purposely to have avoided some
points upon which Niccols dwells, while he has de-

signedly touched others of which Shakespeare availed himself.[1]

Those who read the ensuing pages will very soon perceive that the writer of them was a practised versifier,

---

[1] In Restituta, iv, 15, may be seen specimens of a manuscript poem on "the Rising to the Crown of Richard the Third," which seems never to have been printed, and which is in distinct imitation of the style of "The Mirror for Magistrates." Three stanzas, referring to the productions of three distinguished poets, Churchyard, Daniel, and Lodge, are worth subjoining.

> " *Shore's Wife*, a subject though a prince's mate,
>   Had little cause her fortune to lament.
> Her birth was meane, and yet she liv'd in state ;
>   The King was dead before her honour went.
> *Shore's Wife* might fall, and none can justly wonder
> To see her fall that useth to lye under.
>
> *Rosamond* was fayre, and far more fayre than she:
>   Her fall was great, and but a woman's fall.
> Tryfles are great compare them but with me ;
>   My fortunes farre were higher then they all.
> I left this land possest with civill strife,
> And lost my crowne, mine honour, and my life.
>
> *Elstred* I pitie, for she was a queene,
>   But for my selfe to sigh I sorrow want :
> Her fall was great, but greater falls have been ;
>   Some falls they have that use the court to haunt.
> A toye did happen, and this queene dismay'd ;
> But yet I see not why she was afrayd."

The dedication of the poem, from which this extract is made, is dated Sep. 4, 1593, and it was prepared for the press though never published: at that date "Shore's Wife" had been written some years by Thomas Churchyard, while Daniel's poem on Rosamond, and Lodge's on Elstred, had only just appeared.

and a man of very considerable poetical power, although his taste may be defective: he sometimes writes below his subject, and at other times the effort to reach the height of it is too evident. Altogether, his work is unequal, and the serious commencement of a stanza is now and then entirely spoiled by the ludicrous conclusion of it: for instance, he thus makes Richard speak of Jane Shore, and of a dramatic performance of which she was the heroine.

> " And what a peece of justice did I shew
>   On Mistresse Shore, when (with a fancied hate
> To unchast life) I forced her to goe
>   Bare-foote, on penance, with dejected state!
> But now her fame by a vile play doth grow,
>   Whose fate the women so commisserate;
>   That who (to see my justice on that sinner)
>   Drinks not her teares, and makes her fast their dinner!"

Here an absurd conceit in the last line is made to mar the whole effect of the preceding part of the stanza. We may add that the " vile play," to which reference is made, was not probably that already reprinted by the Shakespeare Society, " The First and Second Parts of Edward IV," by Thomas Heywood, in which Jane Shore is an important character, but that which is thus mentioned in a poetical tract called " Pymlico, or Run Redcap," published in 1609 :—

> "Amaz'd I stood to see a crowd
> Of civil throats stretch'd out so loud :
> As at a new play, all the rooms
> Did swarm with gentles, mix'd with grooms,
> So that I truly thought all these
> Came to see *Shore* or *Pericles*."

This passage seems to settle the point that the plays of " Shore " and of " Pericles " were brought out at about the same date, neither of them perhaps absolutely " a new play," as the author of " Pymlico " terms them, but a revival, with additions and alterations, of older dramatic performances, to which so much of novelty was given as to lead the play-going public to consider them new. The prose novel, founded upon " Pericles," before mentioned, was printed in 1608, no doubt while the play was maintaining an extraordinary degree of popularity. Some account of it may be found in vol. viii., pp. 267, 268, 269, of the edition of Shakespeare published by Messrs. Whittaker and Co.; and larger extracts are given from it in " Farther Particulars regarding Shakespeare and his Works," (of which only fifty copies were printed) pp. 33 *et seq.*

In his " Epistle to the Reader," the author of " The Ghost of Richard the Third " mentions the popularity of plays upon the events of that reign: " And when I undertook this, I thought with myself that to draw arguments of invention from the subject, new and probable, would be far more plausible to the time, than by insisting upon narrations, *made so common in plays* and so notorious among all men, have my labour slighted and my pen taxed for trivial." The fact is, that besides Dr. Legge's Latin drama, (acted at Cambridge before 1583) in 1614 there were at least three existing English plays upon the story of Richard III. The oldest of these no doubt was " The True Tragedie of Richard the Third," (written several years earlier, and printed in 1594) which preceded Shakespeare's historical drama,[1] which we suppose to have been composed about 1593. Shakespeare's historical drama, therefore, came second in point of date; and on the 22nd of June, 1602, Ben Jonson was paid £10 by Henslowe, in earnest of a play to be called " Richard Crook-back," and of some additions to Kyd's " Spanish Tragedy." We know, from the impression of " The Spanish Tragedy " in 1602, that the additions by Ben Jonson were not very important; so that we may presume that the larger part of the £10 advanced by Henslowe went to pay for what Ben Jonson had already written of his " Richard Crook-back." At about this date, £10 or £12 seems to have been the price usually given for a complete play; and it is likely that, at the time he received the money, Ben Jonson was far advanced in his undertaking, and that it was afterwards finished, and acted by Henslowe and Alleyn's company at the Fortune Theatre, which had been opened not long before. As it was written in 1602, it may appear singular that Ben Jonson did not include his " Richard Crook-back " in the folio of his Works in 1616; but it is probable that he was aided in the play by some other dramatist, and several pieces in which he was notoriously concerned were excluded from that volume, because, having had partners in them, he could not term them exclusively his own. " Sejanus " would have been in this predicament, had not Ben Jon-

---

[1] An accurate reprint of "The True Tragedy of Richard the Third," 1594, from the unique copy in the collection of the Duke of Devonshire, has just been issued by the Council of the Shakespeare Society: to it is appended the Latin drama upon the same subject by Dr. Legge, from the MS. in the Library of Emmanuel College.

son re-written that portion which he admits had been contributed by a "happy genius;" meaning, as has been always supposed, Shakespeare.

What we have just stated proves that there were at least three English dramas of which Richard was the hero, viz., " The true Tragedy," Shakespeare's historical play, and Ben Jonson's " Richard Crook-back." These, we may presume, were more or less in a course of performance, in 1614, when " The Ghost of Richard the Third " was published, although the old " True Tragedy " may have been superseded by the later productions of Shakespeare and Ben Jonson : other theatres, besides the Globe and Fortune, may have been in possession of plays upon the same incidents; but none such have come to our day, nor any notices regarding them.

The only remaining point to which it seems necessary to advert is the question, Who was the author of " The Ghost of Richard the Third?" No name or initials are found on the title-page, but the letters C. B. are appended to the dedication : these may belong to Charles Best, who was a writer in Davison's " Poetical Rhapsody," 1602, or to Christopher Brooke, the author of some " Eglogues dedicated to his much loved friend Mr. Will. Browne," printed in the same year as the poem before us. It will be observed that Browne has lines in commendation of his " worthy and ingenious friend, the author," prefixed to " The Ghost of Richard the Third," as well as similar poems by George Chapman, George Wythers (or Wither), Robert Daborne, and Ben Jonson, and four Latin verses by Fr. Dynne, of the Inner Temple.

We are, therefore, more disposed to assign "The Ghost of Richard the Third" to Brooke than to Best, to whom we formerly thought it might possibly be attributed.[1] It is also to be remarked, that Christopher Brooke has a laudatory sonnet prefixed to Browne's "Britannia's Pastorals," printed in folio about 1613, in which year the address "to the Reader" is dated. From this work we quote the subsequent tribute to Brooke, forming part of song 2, of book ii., in the impression of 1625, 8vo.

——————— "Brooke, whose polisht lines
Are fittest to accomplish high designes,
Whose pen (it seemes) still young Apollo guides;
Worthy the forked hill for ever glides
Streames from thy braine, so faire, that time shall see
Thee honour'd by thy verse, and it by thee.
And when thy temple's well-deserving bayes
Might impe a pride in thee to reach thy praise,
As in a crystall glasse, fill'd to the ring
With the cleare water of as cleare a spring,
A steady hand may very safely drop
Some quantity of gold, yet o're the top
Not force the liquor run, although before
The glasse (of water) could containe no more;
Yet so all-worthy Brooke, though all men sound
With plummet of just praise thy skill profound,
Thou in thy verse those attributes canst take,
And not apparent ostentation make,
That any second can thy verses raise,
Striving as much to hide as merit praise."

[1] We owe the suggestion that Christopher Brooke was the author of "The Ghost of Richard the Third" to Mr. Rodd.

There was, therefore, an obvious, and probably an intimate, connexion between Christopher Brooke and William Browne; and perhaps the fact of his authorship was so well understood at the time, that Brooke did not consider it necessary to put more than his initials to the poem contained in the ensuing pages. We thought at one time of printing Brooke's "Eglogues" and scattered poems with "The Ghost of Richard the Third," but they are totally unconnected in style and manner, and do not in any way illustrate each other: besides, the authorship of Brooke to the production here reprinted is too uncertain to warrant the annexation of his avowed works. Little seems to be known of him beyond what is said by Browne, and the fact that he was an author of some distinction in the time of Shakespeare. Whether he were descended from Arthur Brooke, the author of the narrative poem of "Romeus and Juliet," first published in 1562, has never been ascertained.

We have to thank Dr. Bandinel, curator of the Bodleian Library, for permission to transcribe "The Ghost of Richard the Third;" and Mr. Harper, for the trouble he took in collating the transcript, in order to make sure that our re-impression represents, verbally and literally, the text of the *unique* original. Of course, mere typographical errors are corrected in the text, or pointed out in the notes.

THE

GHOST

OF

RICHARD

THE THIRD.

Expressing himselfe in these three Parts

{
1 *His Character*
2 *His Legend*
3 *His Tragedie*

Containing more of him then hath been heretofore shewed;
either in Chronicles, Playes, or Poems.

Laurea Desidiœ prœbetur nulla.

Printed by G. Eld: for L. Lisle: and are to be sold
in Paules Church-yard at the signe of the
Tygers head. 1614.

TO THE RIGHT WORSHIPFULL SIR JOHN CROMPTON, KNIGHT; WITH HIS MOST WORTHY LADY, THE LADY FRANCES.

Sir,

My simple disposition could never make cunning observance of any whose deserts most bound me to their respect and honor, not more out of my nature then judgement, since commonly the world's obsequious insinuations in trifles prove their obsequies of no more importance. Nor can the weightiest duties, in my poore habilities, sway much more the ballance of the world, because the notice that the world takes of men's noble loves to vertue and good name impresseth nothing the more, but oftentimes their lesse price in onely profit and selfe-loving estimations. Notwithstanding, since I know your true noblesse out of the common way in all honored inclination to the acceptance and grace of goodnes, I have beene bold to publish this poem (intending allurement to goodnes by deterring from her contrarie) to your right generous countenance and gracefull protection : wherein, least a single and consortlesse disposition might perhaps grow cold by the too many companions that encourage the death of it to all respect of unprofitable vertue, you have taken into your bosome so free and gratious a love to it in my most honor'd lady, that the comfortable and nourishing flame of it can never want fuell to maintaine and keep it ever at full. To both whose one-light, for the direction and progression of all good endeavors, belonging and consecrate to all true worthines and dignitie, I offer this well-meaning materiall, hoping that such as have no matter to judge it, shall bee farre from enclining your apprehensions to condemne it, and rather establish then diminish in you vertues encreasing encouragement. To which, in all resolv'd service, I humbly submit, ever abiding, and desiring to my utmost your most respected commandement.

C. B.

THE EPISTLE TO THE READER.

An Epistle to the reader is as ordinary before a new book as a prologue to a new play ; but as plaies are many times exploded, though the prologue be never so good and promising, so, reader, if thou findest not stuffe in this poem to fit thy humor, if the wit with the fashion hold not some tollerable proportion, this enducement, though nere so formall and obsequious, would little prevaile with thy acceptation, but thou wouldst conjure my ghost downe againe before his time, or torment him upon earth with the hell-fire of thy displeasure : therefore, it matters not whether I humor thee with complement, or insinuate with glozing epithites.   I knowe (in a play or poem) thou lik'st best of satyricall stuffe, though perhaps thou seest therein thine own character : and not without some shew of reason are things bitter the better ; for the gluttonous sences (the eye and eare) so cloi'd and surfeited with variety of effeminate pleasures, the rough satyre doth sometimes not unfitly enterpose such courtly delight, which growing a burthen to it selfe, his enter-mixt vaine, with the others vanity, gives entermission to the humor, and proves no lesse tastfull to the gallants judgement then tart sauce to whet his dull'd appetite.   And of this kind I have enterlaced something, naturally rising out of my subject ; where, by way of prevention, if any shall object that I have not amplified the legend to the full scope of the story, I answere, I should then have made the volume too great, to the discouragement of the buyer, and disadvantage of the printer : let it suffice I have the substance if not the circumstance.   And when I undertook this I thought with myselfe, that to draw arguments of invention from the subject, new, and probable, would be farre more plaucible to the time, then by insisting upon narrations, made so common in playes and so notorious among all men, have my labour slighted, and my pen tax't for triviall. The generous censor, as hee is ingenious or ingenuous, I reverence; likewise the crittick, as he is knowing and learn'd, but when his censure shall be levell'd with neither of his good parts, but savour more of spleene then braine, of disease then judgement, I doe hartily appeale from him with all of that faction. And though many did inly wish that this, not the meanest issue of my braine, might have prov'd an obortive, and seene no comfortable light, yet they see it is borne, and without prejudice to nature with teeth, too, to oppose theirs, that shall open their lips to deprave mee, but whether to lye upon the parish or the printers hand, that rests in clouds : howsoever, I have got sheetes to lye in (though they be but course) and am sure to be cherish't in good letters : if I be en-tertain'd in the world, and prove a companion for the many, I know I shall not be much chargeable; if not, yet this is my comfort, there will be some use made of me in this land of waste. In which resolution I set up my rest.

Thine, if thou wilt.

TO HIS INGENUOUS AND MUCH-LOV'D
FRIEND, THE AUTHOR.

You now amids our Muses Smithfield are,
To sell your Pegasus, where hackney ware
(Rid by the swish swash rippiers of the time,
Pamper'd and fronted with a ribband ryme)
Though but some halfe houre soundly try'd, they tyre,
Yet sell, as quickned with eternall fire.
All things are made for sale ; sell man and all,
For sale, to hell : there is no soule to sale.
Your flippant sence-delighter, smooth and fine,
Fyr'd with his bush muse and his sharpe hedge wine,
Will sell like good old Gascoine.   What does, then,
Thy purple in graine with these red-oker men?
Swarth chimney sweepe, that to his horne doth sing,
More custome gets, then in the Thespian spring
The thrice-bath'd singer to the Delphian lyre.
Though all must needs be rid heere, yet t'aspire
To common sale, with all turne-serving jades,
Fits pandars, and the strong voic't fish-wife trades.
Affect not that then, and come welcome forth,
Though to some few, whose welcom's somthing worth.
Not one, not one (sayes Perseus) will reade mine ;
Or two, or none : 'tis pageant orsadine
That goes for gold in your barbarian rate,
You must be pleas'd, then, to change gold for that.
Might I be patterne to the meanest few,
Even now, when hayres of women-hated-hew

Are wither'd on me, I delight to see
My lines thus desolately live like me,
Not any thing I doe but is like nuts
At th' ends of meales left, when each appetite gluts.
Some poet yet can levell you a verse
At the receipt of custome, that shall pierce
A sale assister ; as if with one eye   ⎫
He went a burding, strikes fowles as they fly, ⎬
And has the very art of foulerie :   ⎭
Which art you must not envie ; be you pleas'd
To hit desert ; fly others, as diseas'd,
Whose being pierst is but to be infected ;
And as bold Puritans (esteem'd elected)
Keep from no common plague, which so encreases ;
So these feed all poeticall diseases.
Best ayre, lest dwellers hath ; yet thinke not I
Fore-speake the sale of thy sound poesie,
But would, in one so worth encouragement,
The care of what is counted worst prevent ;
   And with thy cheerefull going forth with this,
   Thy Muse in first ranke of our Muses is.
            Non datur ad Musas currere lata via.
               GEOR : CHAPMAN.

TO HIS WORTHY AND INGENIOUS FRIEND,

THE AUTHOR.

So farre as can a swayne (who then a rounde
   On oaten-pipe no further boasts his skill)
I dare to censure the shrill trumpets sound,
   Or other musick of the Sacred Hil :
The popular applause hath not so fell,
   (Like Nile's lowd cataract) possest mine eares,

But others songs I can distinguish well,
  And chant their praise despis'd vertue reares:
Nor shall thy buskind Muse be heard alone
  In stately pallaces; the shady woods
By me shall learn't, and eccho's one by one
  Teach it the hils, and they the silver floods.
Our learned shepheards, that have us'd tofore
  Their happy gifts in notes that wooe the plaines,
By rurall ditties will be knowne no more,
  But reach at fame by such as are thy straines.
And I would gladly, (if the Sisters' spring
  Had me inabled) beare a part with thee,
And for sweet groves, of brave heroes sing;
  But since it fits not my weake melodie,
    It shall suffice that thou such meanes do'st give,
    That my harsh lines among the best may live.
                    W. BROWNE.
                        Int: Temp.

AD LECTOREM DE LIBRO.

Hic nihil invenies quod carpas: mentior; ecquid
  Carpere quod pigeat, tam bonus hortus habet?
Hinc carpat, quisquis gratos vult carpere flores;
  At dextrà carpat, carpere si quis amat.
                    FR. DYNNE. *Int: Temp.*

TO HIS FRIEND THE AUTHOR, UPON
HIS POEM.

Not for thy love to me, nor other merit,
Doe I commend thy poem's forme or spirit;

For though I know thou art a friend of mine,
I praise this for it owne sake, not for thine.
Here have I seen character'd the condition,
The life and end of a meere polititian ;
From which I learne, 'tis no good policy
On any termes to part with honesty.
And the opprest may view, (to his content)
How sweet it is to be an innocent ;
Or by contraries learne, with what deare rest
The soules of harmelesse dying men are blest.
So may the bloody tyrant heere attend,
What horror and despaire pursues his end.
And those that (living) loath their faults to heare,
May (reading this) perhaps repent for feare ;
    Since though reproofes they scorne now here they dwell,
    Thus their owne Ghosts proclaime their shames from hell.

GEORGE WYTHERS.

TO THE AUTHOR, UPON HIS POEM.

I know thou art too knowing to enquire
This title to thy praise, which doth require
A hart so constant, and a brow so chast,
That vertue must not fall, how e're low plac't :
Who this way merits best must looke to bring
Onely a flower to an intemp'rate spring ;
Which howsoe're with care thy labor plants,
Must feele the earth-bred blasts in barren wants,
Of ruder elements oft suffring spoile,
To shew such hearbs grow not on naturall soile ;
Nor can't be aptlier said of verse and rimes,
They are but strangers to these wav'ring times :

For, as men shift their fashions for new shapes,
They are in soules the same (inconstant apes)
Which each booke-seller knowes ; for, as to day,
Your Pasquil like a mad-cap runnes away,
To morrow playes ; the next day history ;
More strange, another time divinitie ;
And in my age (which is indeed most rare)
I have knowne gallants buy up bookes of prayer ;
But they were gamsters, loosing all in swearing,
Try'd a contrarie way in their uprearing.
To this my common observation, thou
Hast tooke a course (which I must needs allow),
T' include them all in one, to catch their eyes,
That soone are dym'd without varieties ;
Wherein I will not flatter thee to tell,
There's much of good, and what is worst is well.

ROBERT DABORNE.

TO HIS FRIEND THE AUTHOR, UPON
HIS RICHARD.

When these, and such, their voices have employd,
    What place is for my testimony void ?
Or, to so many, and so broad-seales had,
    What can one witnesse, and a weake one, add
For such a worke, as could not need theirs ?   Yet
    If praises, when th' are full, heaping admit,
My suffrage brings thee all increase, to crowne
    Thy Richard, rais'd in song past pulling downe.

BEN JONSON.

THE

GHOST OF RICHARD

THE THIRD.

HIS CHARACTER.

What magick, or what fiend's infernall hand,
   Reares my tormented ghost from Orcus flame,
And lights my conscience with her burning brand,
   Through death and hell to view the world's faire frame?
Must I againe regreete my native land,
   Whose graves resound the horror of my name?
     Then gaspe those marble jawes, and birds of night
     Perplex my passage to the loathed light.

Some consciences, with soules, may hope for peace
   When all their veniall and their petty crimes
Are expiate, but mine will never cease;
   T' augment my torment past all worlds and times,
Damn'd deeds in life, damn'd pennance doth encrease.
   Men's soules may fly their bodies' putrid clymes,
     But horrid paines still cleave to foule offence;
     Nor will the sinne forsake the conscience.

Give way, Time's pageants, bubbles but a blast,
  Objects for idle spirits, whose vanitie
Feede streames of humors in this sea of waste ;
  Where carpet courtlings swim in bravery.
Such comick puppets are not things to last,
  Subjects unfit for fame or memory ;
    But time, nor age, can paralell or stayne
    My bloudy scenes, which Death hath dyde in grayne.

Vale, Nature's nurselings, Fortune's favorites,
  Whose percell guylt my touch will not endure ;
Fostrers of fooles and glib-tongu'd parasites,
  Sick of time's lethargie, past hope of cure ;
Cameleons in your change of gaudy sights ;
  How wanton Salmasis, with lust impure,
    Cleaves to your soules ! proves ye of two fold kind—
    Male in the body, female in the mind !

Wallow in wast, still jet in sumptuous weeds,
  Wave, feathered gulls, with wind, and shrinck with raine ;
Buskin'd ye are, but not for lofty deeds ;
  No stately matter e'ere inspyr'd your braines ;
Nought but soft love your great ambition feeds :
  None sencible of pleasure, but of paine,
    Must looke on me ; such whose high thoughts are fed
    With spirit, and fame, from dust of bodies dead.

Thinke ye that graves and hollow vaultes inherit
  Nought but oblivion and impotence ?
Doth not from death arise an other spirit,
  Of high resolve th' extracted quintessence ?
Fame is the agent to substantiall merit,
  And beares about the world's circumference
    All deeds notorious which Time remembers ;
    Thus, phœnix-like, life springs from down-trod embers.

Then, as th' Almighty Thunderer doth shake
  (With selfe-bred fumes) th' immense and massie earth,
No lesse amazement may my fury make
  In my live's horror, from my monstrous byrth.
And since I'm raised from hell's burning lake,
  Ile fright the world, and chase all formes of mirth
    From this now mimick and ridiculous stage :
    I sing of murther, tyrany, and rage.

Then, let the canker'd trumpets of the deepe
  Proclaime my entrance to this stagie round,
That I may startle worldlings from their sleepe,
  Their sences in security fast bound.
My tongue in firie dragons' spleene I steepe,
  That acts with accents cruelty may sound ;
    As once the furies' snakes hist in my breath,
    When I kist horror, and engender'd death.

And that my devilish braine may not be dull,
  But touch the quick of each ambitious soule,
I take the wittiest pollitician's skull,
  That ever hell's black booke did yet enroule ;
His mazor fill'd with Stygian juice brym-full,
  And innocent blood, fit for an ebon bowle,
    I quaffe to all damn'd spirits, and I know well
    They'l pledg me, though they drinke as deepe as hell.

All yee, then, that are flesh't in tyranny,
  View me, your ruthlesse president and mirror.
Now all earth's glew'd together villany
  Dissolve and melt with pale and gastly terror :
Loe ! I unclaspe the booke of Memory,
  Rowze, bed-rid age, fowle sinne, and smooth fac'd error ;
    And with all these awake, Antiquity,
    To sing my actions to posterity.

In my conception, nature strove with kinde,
　When, in the heate of blood and lust's desire,
Imagination mov'd (a part of mind),
　And with the seede commixt an ardent fire;
A strange effect, these powres should be combyn'd,
　The mortall with th' immortall part conspire
　　To forme a prodegy the world to fright,
　　To blemish humanes, and distayne the light.

For why? My mother, in the strength of thought,
　Propos'd unto her apprehensive powre
Some monstrous birth, by nature's error wrought,
　On which all plannets of good luck did lowre:
My syre corruption to this fancy brought.
　My mother languish't many a tedious houre;
　　Travell brought sweate and grones; shee long'd to see
　　Her burth'nous fraught: at last she brought forth me.

My legges came formost, an unequall payre,
　Much like the badgers, that makes swiftest speede
In waies uneven: which shew'd that no course faire
　Should crowne my life and actions to succeed:
Hollow my cheekes, upon my brest black hayre,
　The characters of spleene and virulent deeds;
　　My beetle-brow, and my fire-cyrcled eye,
　　Foreshew'd me butcher in my cruelty.

Then, as a brow-bent hill, much undermin'd,
　Casts scowling shadowes o're the neighb'ring plaines,
Which th' approchers feare, as being enclyn'd
　To bury all his spatious reach containes,
So, mountaine-like was I contract behind,
　That my stretch't armes (plumpe with ambitious veines)
　　Might crush all obstacles, and throw them downe,
　　That stood betwixt my shadow and a crowne.

And as a raven's beake, pointed to the south,
    Crokes following ill, from sharpe and rav'nous maw;
Such cry Yorkes bird sent from a fatall mouth,
    Boading confusion to each wight I saw.
To adde to these, (as token of more ruth)
    Th' amazed women started; for each jaw
        Appear'd with teeth : which mark made these ils
           good,
        That I should woorry soules, suck humane blood.*

My father rav'd, my mother curst her wombe,
    Th' impris'ned winds shooke earth, and burst their
        caves ;
And time (swolne big with sad events to come)
    Did send forth throes, eccho'd by gasping graves :
The lights of heaven dropt on the world's darke tombe ;
   Horror invades the maine, whose raging waves
        Doe foame, and swell above their bounds (the earth).
        These fatall signes raign'd at my fearefull byrth.

In progresse of my childhood, with delight
    I taught my nature to see fowles to bleede ;
Then, at the slaughter-house, with hungry sight,
    Upon slaine beasts my sensuall part did feede ;
And (that which gentler natures might affright)
    I search't their entrayles, as in them to reade
        (Like th' ancient bards) what fate should thence
           betide,
        To cherish sin and propagate my pride.

* The hardning of a humane nature in bloud; alluding to this of
Plutarch : Ab initio noxium animal devoratum fuit: deinde avis aliqua
donec his condoce facta, et gustui adsueta libido ad bouē operarium pro-
gressa est: Itaq paulatim in expletam roborātes auiditatem, in cœdes ho-
minum et bella sunt delapsi.

C

Then (as I waxed in maturity)
  I would frequent the sessions, and those places
Where guilty men receiv'd their doomes to dye;
  As well to note the gestures and the graces
Of those were cast, as of the judge's eye;
    How these looke pale; the others front out-faces
      Eene death itselfe: and hence I learned how
      To conquer pitty with a bended brow.

Now (to confirme these notions in my braine,
  And to chase thence all naturall formes of good)
To presse to executions sooth'd my vaine,
  To see men reeking in their sweate and bloud:
O, how remorslesse was I of their paine!
  It was my cordiall and my nourishing food.
    These ruthles thoughts were in my hart so rife,
    That I could laugh at death, and sport with life.

As butchers and loath'd hang-men in their life,
  (Through bent of mind and instrumentall partes)
Being often us'd unto the bloody knife,
  Make blood and death the habits of their harts;
·And therefore, since with them such acts are rife,
  The lawes of kinde (in lieu of their deserts)
    Exempted have from life and death's sterne jewries,
    Who for their natures might well ranke with furies.

So this habituall custome ever breeds
  Such fixt impression in th' affects and sence,
That thence the minde receaves corruptive seedes;
  Nor doth sincerely take the difference
'Twixt cruell actions and compassionate deeds:
  So man and beast, with guylt and innocence,
    Are all alike to tyrants in their swayes,
    Where sensuall will commands, and not obaies.

Thus, as contagious ayre breeds some disease,
    Which all unseene creeps on in fowle infection,
Till at the last the vitall parts it ceaze,
    And in his mortall kind attaines perfection ;
So by corruption of such thoughts as these,
    And giving way to humor and affection,
        Pernitious ills encreas'd ; and thus I found
        How pitty lost and cruelty won her ground.

Now, for I knew great spirits in ignorance
    Were farre unfit to sway, or to command,
Since cunning arts do pollitick ends advance,
    I sought to joyne their strengths into one band,
And (t'arme myselfe against the threats of chance)
    I gave myselfe corruptly t'understand
        Letters and artes, whose superficiall skill
        Might lay the ground to propagate my ill.

Hence were my organs apt, and parts dispos'd
    To give my intellect the formes of things ;
Hence was the chaos of my braine disclos'd.
    That through each sence convei'd their hidden springs :
Their winding streames yet in my sea were cloz'd,
    Which made me swell in state, and surge with kings ;
        Yet with no lyne or plummet to be sounded,
        Nor in no limit but a crowne be bounded.

In my designes I bore no wexen face,
    To take the print of any formes within ;
I had a forge that temper'd it like brasse ;
    Nor by my tongue my hart was knowne or seene ;
Betweene these two there was so ample space,
    That words and thoughts were never of a kin :
        With threats I could allure, smile when I fround,
        Kisse when I kil'd, and heale when I did wound.

From schoole-men's customes I observ'd some skill.
  What's their nice learning and their wrangling strife,
But gaine, or glory, to turne good to ill ?
  As if from reason passion we derive.
Then since these ends in sciences raigne still,
    And few professe them for an after life,
      As they tooke swindge then from their polliticke schools,
      So I tooke licence from their positive rules.

What Midas toucht turnd gould, such learnings use,
  For like the spider, and industrious bee,
What one makes good the other turnes t'abuse ;
  Such was the nature of my subtilty :
With good and ill so play'd I fast and loose,
    Converting things of most indifferency
      To the peculiar habit of my minde,
      And to my forecast thought all others blinde.

I did allow of colledges and schooles,
  And learn'd their logicall distinction,
Yet I perceav'd the greatest clarkes but fooles,
  In judgement rawe, weake in prevention :
I heard their lectures, could digest their rules,
    And make good use of their division ;
      Yet, like to wards, in nonage still I held them,
      Though they were witty, yet could wisdom weild them.

Religion I profest, as most men saw,
  But in my hart deny'd it reverence ;
For I esteem'd it as a penall law,
  To curb and keepe men in obedience :
Yet from her grounds such notions I would drawe,
    To touch my wished poynt of eminence,
      That I in others would exact her breach,
      As great ones in their lyves such doctrine teach.

Arts raise their collumnes upon natures bases ;
   And but observe and play what shee propounds,
And every act of science enterlaces
   Humors and mirth among their scænes profound ;
But cunning onely is the art that graces,
   And most affects, in this conspicuous round ;
      Which having shewne, with fame we part the stage,
      And others enter mov'd with selfe same rage.

I saw it was a worke of natures kind,
   Ambitiously to prick men on to state ;
By force or cunning to make way, or wind
   Through any course, whose end might make them great :
Humanity by good sence I did finde
   To be compact of powre and slye deceats,
      Proposing rules to our owne wish in fortune ;
      Thus each mans selfe-good did him moste importune.

All ayme at welth or pompe, so catch at fame,
   Vertu's invisible, therefore not knowne ;
Few love her for herselfe, but for her name.
   Yet what's without us we would have our owne ;
And honor, being usurp't by vertues clayme,
   Seemes but an accident in vertue growne :
      If accidents by substance only live,
      Take vertue from us, what can honor give ?

I was not one of vertues fond approvers,
   That courted her imaginary face ;
I saw her servants and her doting lovers
   Were poore, and bare, exempt from state or place :
I saw that he, her collours that discovers,
   And beares th' opinion only of her grace,
      Did make most shew with truth to be entyre ;
      To be is vaine, to seeme men most desire.

It was not in my daies, as once of old,
 When vertue had the worlds faire emperie,
Then was that innocent time, the age of gold,
 Whose coyne was truth, whose stampe integrity :
Now monies love proves us of baser mould,
  For as the ages fell successively
   From gold to silver, thence to brasse, now worse,
   So men translate their chiefe good to the purse.

He that insinuates with pollicy,
 That hats and harts with admiration drawes,
That shadowes tyrannous thoughts with clemency,
 And keepes his height with populare applause,
Intytles goodnesse with prosperity,
  And makes his acts authenticall as lawes,
   Proves actions fortunate, though nere so vile,
   To get the type of fame and vertues style.

Then each mans deeds hath praise, his actions grace,
 If squar'd by forme, and rul'd by imitation,
And honor, got by blood, by wealth, or place,
 Will hold his die if glost by ostentation ;
But where both truth and colours want, all's base,
  Then, if we use the vertue most in fashion,
   Honor attends us, grace will never swerve :
   All strive to have, but few men to deserve.

Colours, not truth, then winne the worlds reward,
 For like th' obsequious mercenary minde,
Few love the merrit, all affect reward,
 And so for currant counterfeits are coyn'd ;
Then no ascent so steepe, no doore so bar'd,
  But he that with deceite the world can blinde,
   May make his way, though stradling in his gate,
   Through heads uncover'd to the chayre of state.

And such was I : for wit and fortune make
   Crooked things straite, to these opinion cleaves ;
Which alchimy for currant golde doth take,
   And like the busie spynner ever weaves
Slight webs of praise, and all for greatnesse sake :
   And thus we see how slye deceite deceaves
      The credulous route, whose suffrage, though but breath,
      Yet from that ayre greatnesse takes life, or death.

Proud of this knowledge, I scru'd into the state,
   And of that nature got intelligence ;
There saw I publike fortunes, private hate,
   In severall tempers of impatience.
One stirres too soone, and brings on his hard fate,
   Others subdue with time and providence ;
      Some mixe their blouds to gaine thē powerfull friends,
      And by that meanes worke safest to their ends.

I saw in friendship vertue best did suite,
   In factions powre ; and the most pollitick head,
Since it can only plot, not execute,
   With meaner fortunes best was seconded ;
Some wise, some valiant, some of base repute,
   And all like severall simples tempered,
      Which, well prepar'd by a projecting braine,
      Give greatnesse strength, ambitious hopes maintaine.

I noted statesmen in their agitations,
   How they dispatched suters that implor'd them,
The followers of their fortunes and their fashions,
   How like to demy-gods they did adore them ;
I saw (in offer'd cause of severall passions)
   With what unmoved countenance they bore them :
      Griefe cast not downe, joy spritned not their eyes ;
      Rage bent no brow, their very feare seem'd wise.

This taught my spleene should never ope too fast,
    That polici's not sound if full of poares;
What's violent in ambition will not last;
    The foord is shallow'st where the channell roares.
I saw by them 'twas vaine to spend my blast;
    For first we must take in, then shut the doores,
      And but by secret posterns to convey
      Our aymes by close and undiscover'd way.

I learn'd, likewise, t' appease an enemy
    In termes without hostility and warre;
To win an agent without jealousie,
    And make him tractable and regular;
To hold affection in confederacy
    Without expense; and to prevent or barre
      Seditious tumults without violence,
      And keepe men longing still in patience.

To get close friends about a forraine prince,
    To further home designes with secresie,
And (to relieve the private state expense)
    Make publique purses fill the treasurie:
In this they us'd Nature's intelligence;
    That, as the clouds do render plenteously
      The sunne exhaled steames to earth's encrease,
      So subjects change base drosse for welthy peace.

This is the wisedome (saith the ancient sawe)
    That rules the stars, outworkes the wheele of chance;
And from this modell did I seeke to draw
    Sound principles, my hopes with haps t'advance:
And as ill manners first made soundest law,
    So these instructions, chasing ignorance,
      Mine owne corrupt ends prompted me t' acquire,
      Not lawes to curb, but groundworkes to aspire.

Also in counsell I observ'd and noted,
  How Philautia's sort tooke fire and blase
From others' light, whose innocent margents quoted
  From their originals did win them praise ;
How some by grace sat ; some againe that doted
  Through feeble age (yet trac'd in politick wayes)
    Could help defects, and see with others' eyes,
    Extract their wits, and make themselves seeme wise.

These (like the others) labor'd not to sound
  The depth of things ; but, fraught with burthen light,
They sayl'd more shallow, neere unto the ground,
  And, at the tyde's returne, discharg'd their freight.
In quest of glorie all their strengths were bound :
  Not matter, but the circumstance more sleight
    They touch't at still, whose main entents and hopes
    Were to involve their aymes in sounder scopes.

Yet did this mixture of varietie
  (Like melting hayle, and sollid pearle, or stone)
Seeme like the elements in qualitie,
  Assembled by a disproportion ;
For, as their jars worke on humanitie,
  And make sweet musick in confusion,
    So states-men, join'd in one, unlike in parts,
    One body prove, one life in severall harts.

But, as the planets have a proper sway,
  And move to heav'n (that turnes them) contrarie,
So I from all drew a peculiar way
  To right myselfe 'gainst nature's injurie ;
For since she so mishap't my bodie's clay,
  I labor'd in my minde's deformitie
    To mock her worke : she made me like to none,
    Therefore I thought to be my selfe alone.

And as your-selfe lov'd politicks n'ere care
  What tempests vulgar vessels doe betide,
So that their mighty argoses may share
  Their ruin'd states, made prize unto their pride;
So in the ship of state my selfe did fare,
  (Driv'n with ambition's gale and swelling tyde)
    I forst no publique wrack, no private fall,
    So I might rule and raigne sole lord of all.

Thus have I character'd my spirit and state
  In generall termes; next shall yee heare apply'd
The sequell of mine actions to that fate
  Which heaven ordain'd, as justice to my pride.
This my præludium, now I must relate
  My life, in horrid sinnes diversifi'd:
    There note how saile-hoyst barks incurre a shelfe,
    When greatnes would be greater then itselfe.

FINIS.

THE

LEGEND OF RICHARD THE THIRD.

To him that impt my fame with Clio's quill,
  Whose magick rais'd me from oblivion's den,
That writ my storie on the Muses' hill,
  And with my actions dignifi'd his pen ;
He that from Helicon sends many a rill,
  Whose nectared veines are drunke by thirstie men ;
    Crown'd be his stile with fame, his head with bayes,
    And none detract, but gratulate his praise.

Yet if his scænes have not engrost all grace
  The much fam'd action could extend on stage ;
If time, or memory, have left a place
  For me to fill, t' enforme this ignorant age,
To that intent I shew my horrid face,
  Imprest with feare, and characters of rage :
    Nor wits, nor chronicles, could ere containe
    The hell-deepe reaches of my soundlesse braine.

Then heare, ambitious men, soules drown'd in sences,
  And ever dry in quenchles thirst of glory ;
And yee that have no eares (yee heartes of princes)
  Measure your pompe by processe of my story :
There is a fate your boundles hope convinces,
  Though nought confine yee in this transitory ;
    Those that clime high in mischeefe, rip'st of all,
    Have still the feareful'st and most rotten fall.

What time my father York began his claime,
   Whence civill and uncivill armes did grow,
When purple gore deaw'd many a fertile plaine,
   And swords made furrowes English hearts to sow ;
When sonnes by sires, and sires by sonnes were slaine,
   And England's common-weale a common woe ;
     When heaven rain'd vengeance, and hell sulpher spew'd,
     And every age and sex those sad times rew'd,

I, though too young as then to mannage steele,
   (Yet in my thoughtes the theory of armes)
My swelling veines and feeble nerves did feele
   The emulation of those hot alarms.
My glorie's thirst made appetite so reele
   Betweene my peacefull state and boistrous stormes,
     That, in the heat and fervor of desire,
     I spur'd on nature, and set blood on fire.

My father's sword or title set on foot,
   Whose fate growne ripe he dropt to earth and perish't ;
But we, the sonnes, (greene branches of his roote)
   Th' aspiring vertue of his hopes still cherish't :
I and my brother held in swift poursuit
   The royall game, whose thoughtes were jointly nourish't
     With the possession of that chased prize,
     As for a crowne who would not Nimrodize.

Now (seconded with right and warre's faire merits)
   I mixt my blood with gall, my spleene with ire :
Heere I began to jovialize my spirit,
   Midst thundring shock darting Cyclopian fire.
Fame prickt us on to that we were t' inherit,
   And we made way through blood, nor could retire,
     Till on the rubbish of our enemy
     We reard the ensigne of our victory.

Then was the kingly Lyon * held at bay
  Coopt in the Towre, whose lionesse rag'd in vaine.
To rescue or redeeme our purchast prey
  I pitcht more toyles, wherein her whelp was tane:
Edward, her faire sonne (glory of the day)
  My hand eclipst with foule and bloudy staine;
    A murder, that might make the starres to winke,
    The fixed poles to shake, and Atlas shrinke.

Next (to secure our parts from Henrie's side)
  The dy being bar'd, the chance fell on the maine,
And damned policie instructed pride
  To stretch my conscience to a higher straine:
The divell whisper'd, that my hands not dyde
  In Henrie's gore, my hope to rise was vaine.
    My sword's sharpe point brought his *quietus est*,
    Which, level'd to his hart, sent him to rest.

Hence cruell thoughts tooke roote, and overspred
  My syn-manur'd soyle, nature's shapelesse frame:
The ground grew ranke, with blood and murder fed,
  And fearelesse impudence check't blushing shame.
I cherish't tyranny, strooke pittie dead;
  My rage, like salamander, liv'd in flame,
    And, ev'n as drinke doth keep the dropsie dry,
    So more I drunke the more desire did fry.

Yet now (secure) Edward enjoy'd the crowne.
  Warre's sterne alarums heere began to cease;
Bankes turn'd to pillowes, fields to beds of downe,
  And boystrous armes to silken robes of peace:
Warre's counsellor resum'd the states-man's gowne,
  And welcom'd blisse grew big with all encrease;
    Wealth follow'd peace, and ease succeeded plenties,
    And needfull bates were turn'd to wanton dainties.

          * Henry the Sixth.

Now Mars his brood were chain'd to women's lockes ;
    Surgeons and leaches us'd for Venus harmes :
They that erst liv'd by wounds now thrive by th' pox,
    For smoothest pleasure still ensues rough armes ;
Whiles I gryn'd like a woolfe, lier'd like a fox,
    To see soft men turn'd swine by Cyrces' charmes ;
       And, being not shap't for love, employ'd my wits
       In subtile wiles, t' exceede these hum'rous fits.

O, how I bit my tongue when Edward wiv'd !
    That (with the rest) forc'd shoutes of God give joy,
When to the center of my hart there div'd
    Curses, and rankorous wishes to destroy ;
My hopes grew dead, yet (hydra-like) surviv'd
    Fresh heads of strength, which mischiefe did employ,
       And my smooth genius sooth'd me in the eare,
       That blood would sanguine the pale cheeke of feare.

Whiles wanton Edward doates on Mistresse Shore,
    Whose lust and tryfling soyld the face of things ;
And counsellors (like pandars) kept the dore,
    My thoughts were climing to the state of kings :
He painted beautie, I did crownes adore,
    And ever impt ambition's ayrie wings,
       To reach at fame and fortune, which might crowne
       Hope with successe, and wit with fame's renowne.

And even as he (with an insatiate sight)
    Beheld a beautious face, a sparkling eye,
Admir'd a pleasant wit (as love's delight)
    And still adored Cupid's deitie,
So I (enflam'd with glorie's appetite) ·
    Did court the shining beames of majestie,
       Priz'd policie, altars to fortune rear'd :
       He study'd to be lov'd, I to be fear'd.

Clarence his life in Fortune's tickle wheele
  Had now a slipperie stand ; for (dreadlesse) he
In sound estate of health began to reele,
  (As nature's powre must yeeld to tyranny)
My adamant had pointed to his steele,
  And subtly drew him to his destinie :
    I had a craft to undermine each state,
    My engines were the instruments of Fate.

For why ? An ignorant wisard, taught by me,
  That never knew a letter in the rowe,
From his spell'd lesson tooke the letter G,
  To work my rising, and his overthrow :
And by a foolish, childish prophesie,
  (As fooles and children still tell all they know)
    Insinuates with the fearefull king that G
    Should put to death his royall progenie.

So harmelesse Clarence superstitiously
  Is sent to close death to the fatall Tower,
But I, that charm'd, fulfill'd the augurie ;
  So polliticks kill farre off with unseene powre,
With sheathed points I wrought my tyranny :
  Thus could I whet, prepare, feed, and devoure,
    Concoct, evacuate, with most nimble hast :
    Blood was my cheare, and other feasts my fast.

So George rid post ; and at his journeye's end
  (To quench his thirst, and coole his bloody sweate)
His gentle host (being my secret friend)
  Did broach a butt t' allay his dangerous heate ;
But so he sow'st him in't, that he did send
  Poore George to rest, in everlasting seate ;
    Yet no tart wine, but malmsey stopt his breath,
    So dyde he not the sharp'st, but sweetest death.

Next, time an other point begins t' attaine,
  When Edward (past the solstice of his yeares)
With necessarie change begins to wayne,
  And I thrust in to undergo his cares :
Life (sencible of pleasure) now feeles paine,
  Earth must to earth, as nature's course out-weares :
    His scene is done, death strikes him to the hart ;
    So parts the stage, and now begins my part.

Now back-steel'd Buckingham I made my friend :
  Him I sustain'd with hope, and fed with ayre,
To further me in my aspyring end ;
  In whom I found will, power, and faithfull care :
I shot the shaft, and he the bowe did bend,
  And both could runne with hound, and hold with hare ;
    And though to crosse his ayme I had a clause,
    Yet strongest agents back the weakest cause.

Next Rivers, Vaughan, Gray, (that stood in light,
  And justly enterpos'd my unjust ayme)
Did feele the vengeance of my fell despite,
  Whose deaths did more secure my lawlesse claime.
Poore simple soules they were to stand for right,
  Not having strength ; for vertue's power is lame :
    'Tis desperate folly to oppose not strong,
    Then sinke with right 'tis better winke at wrong.

So Regent made, protector to the princes,
  Bare heads, bent knees sooth mischiefe, second hope ;
Religious shewes doe cover close pretenses,
  More towres, more titles, are my fancie's scope :
Now I contract my wits, summon my sences,
  To smooth the rugged way, the dores to ope
    That leade to state : the law being in my will,
    I had a licence to make good my ill.

I plaid with law as with a waxen nose,
    Now made it crookt, then straight, then saddle wise :
And its firme brow I bent unto the toes,
    To make a foot-stoole on't for me to rise.
What wisdome stablisht pollicy ore'throwes,
    Corrupts her pure soule, bleares her fairest eyes.
        Law 's a mute female judge : guifts, wit, and tongue,
        Oft prostitute her parts to lust and wrong.

Truth had a tattering stand, I made commander ;
    Tyrants are ever fearefull of the good,
And innocence in vaine opposeth slander :
    Whom I accus'd or censur'd, who withstood ?
My brayne was as an intricate meander,
    Whence horror issu'd and the streames of blood ;
        My soule, like Stix, and Jove might sweare by me,
        As nought more adverse to his deity.

Now whiles I trembled in an agony,
    Sole soveraignty with safest meanes contriving,
My working head (my counsell's consistory)
    Debates how I might raigne, the princes living :
My powers disjoyn'd, and (for security)
    Neither to other a sure hostage giving ;
        But in this doubtfull conflict left me still
        Betweene my reason and my sensuall will.

Reason objects (to countercheck my pride)
    How kings are nature's idols, made of clay :
And though they were by mortalls deified,
    Yet in the grave beggers as good as they :
That sence was slavish, and for man no guide,
    That reason should command, and will obey ;
        And that with all world's pompe and fortune's good,
        We still were nothing else but flesh and blood.

                                                    D

Reason infer'd, men in effect were kings,
  If they could rule themselves, and conquer passion ;
And that desire soar'd with Icarus' wings,
  When it out-script her bounds of limitation ;
That her powre onely could distinguish things,
  Shew what was reall, what but forme and fashion ;
    Suggests, likewise, that man was overthrowne,
    Not more by others flatterie then his owne.

Farther she urg'd, that fortune had no power
  But in men's ignorance, although shee boast
To blesse, or crosse, as shee doth smile or lowre,
  And to make fooles of those shee flatters most ;
That vertue onely was the minde's rich dowre,
  By wealth not bought, by povertie not lost,
    Which who so had not ever purchast losse,
    His pompe was bane, and titles but his crosse.

This reason doth suggest, which I convince,
  And prove those grounds for idle, false, and vaine :
I knew her powre was in decay of sence,
  Which age, not youth, did foster and maintaine ;
And though your sagest morrallists from hence
  Gave humane precepts with much thanklesse paine,
    Such meager wisedome, writ with death-like clawes,
    I held as foolish as your old wives' sawes.

Low thoughts in high-pitch't hopes despaire do bring ;
  And as one walking when the stars appeare,
Night fils his eye, whence shapes of darknes spring,
  And all his thoughts prove visions by his feare ;
But when Aurora set the day on wing,
  And drives the raven-black night from heav'n's bright sphere,
    Then flowers and trees spangled with dewes he spies,
    And worlds of glories glitter in his eyes :

So when great spirits doe shrinke in cloudy feares,
  Loosing their strength, diminishing their pleasures,
Then wealth, and glorie, and what else is theirs,
  In darkest womb doe bury all their treasures;
But when a kingly boldnes them upreares,
    Treading on cloth of state their solemne measures,
      Then doe they graspe (in vigor of their powres)
      The globe and scepter, and kisse heaven with towres.

Now then (quoth I) let tastelesse lines define
  Vertue and her reward in after time,
Richard, thou hast an essence more divine,
  Which glorie's flame hath purg'd from grossest slime;
Crownes be thy objects, and those eares of thine
  Rellish no musick but a sphere-like chime.
    Thus coucht I reason with my eagle's wings:
    If reason rul'd men, then what need of kings?

No; I look't up, nature bid me aspire,
  So taught the firie essence of my soule:
Harts are small things, but infinite in desire,
  Which neither bounds contain'd, nor bars controule:
The flesh is vapor, and the spirit a fire;
    And joviall minds (when these begin t' inroule)
      Do part the drosse, and on the bodie's head
      Dissolve in thunder what his basenes bred.

So on I went in divelish politick wise.
  The yong prince now from safest sanctuarie
A prelate forst, (some such can temporize)
  Who held with fiends t'enfring church libertie:
The child being brought to me, (as 'twas my guize)
  I kist and blest with fein'd sinceritie
    The innocent soule; and therein did fulfill
    The part of Judas, for I meant to kill.

Him with his brother lodg'd I in the Towre,
  A payre ill met to undergoe like fate.
Now wrinckled browes (like skies before a showre)
  Spred gloomy darknes over England's state :
All sought to save, I purpos'd to devoure ;
  My mynes are lay'd, and they prevent too late :
    Counsels divide, and a confused rumor
    Time sent, as throes, unto my swelling tumor.

Now did I use each working instrument :
  Some fyles to take off, some smooth tooles to glaze,
Some serves t'insinuate ; all for close entent
  Wrought one effectuall end in severall wayes :
I was prime mover in this firmament,
  And they, the sphere-like movers to my praise ;
    But Buckingham, my Jupiter of light,
    Whose influence was mirror of my might.

And as the catholick spirit in man applyes
  Each sence and organ to their proper ends,
Useth the hart, the braine, the eares, and eyes,
  And to th' impulsive soule those powers extends ;
So in this pollitick bodie I devise
  By Buckingham, (my spirit) who slackes or bends
    My usefull engins : him I made my hand,
    T' employ his powre with theirs to my command.

Now, good Lord Hastings, great in all men's grace,
  (Of th' adverse faction fautor and chiefe head)
I heav'd at, and remov'd him from his place,
  That so the rest might faint uncomforted :
My blood-hound Catesby foyl'd him in the chase,
  Who, earst by him being rais'd, cherisht, and bred,
    Knowing himselfe too weake to stand for right,
    Proves treacherously wise, and friend to might.

Thus could I saint a divell with a fiend,
  And make one engine other to drive out,
From a mayne faction cull a secret friend,
  To hold with hope, and to prevent with doubt :
I had a powre to breake what would not bend,
  In cautions us'd my sentinell and scoute,
    In jealousie had Argus' hundred eyes,
    And Nero's cruell hart to tyrannize.

How cunningly did Buckingham and I
  Pretend, and set a coulour in the treason
Of Hastings to our lives ! how suddenly
  We butcher'd (without forme of law or reason)
That harmelesse man ! then gull'd simplicitie
  With forced feare, as if at that same season
    Erinnis and the furies had been bent
    To cast their palenes on our damn'd entent ?

And what a peece of justice did I shew
  On Mistresse Shore, when (with a fained hate
To unchast life) I forced her to goe
  Bare-foote, on penance, with dejected state !
But now her fame by a vile play doth grow,
  Whose fate the women so commisserate ;
    That who (to see my justice on that sinner)
    Drinks not her teares, and makes her fast their dinner?

Now, whiles all wish to see yong Edward crown'd,
  And in each place a solemne preparation,
In my vast sea their streames of joy were drown'd,
  Whose ayme was bent to crosse their expectation ;
For Buckingham and I had laid the ground
  To raise my columne, and suppresse their station ;
    And much untemper'd morter was in hand,
    To dawbe and ciment what could never stand.

The gayne and glorie-thirsting smooth divine,
  More learn'd then true, yet of lesse arte then fame,
And many others with him doe combine
  To sleike and pollish my corrupter clayme ;
And whiles their wits doe work to make me shine,
  To guild my guilt, and glorifie my shame,
    Like racking clouds, the people flock and runne,
    With pitchie breathes t' obscure my rising sonne.

But I, that held the conscience but a sawe,
  In my selfe-love confounding idle hate,
Found tricks t' impeach the princes' claime by lawe,
  Proving mine true, theirs illigitimate ;
And to this end subborn'd one Doctor Shaw,
  With servile tongue and spirit adulterate,
    To preach dead Edward's slander with my mother,
    And bastardize the issue of my brother.

.It was suggested then, most impiously,
  Edward nor Clarence to be lawful payres,
But (by th' erronious rule of phisnomy)
  To be the issue of some stranger syres ;
That Edward had, with fowlest bygamy,
  Blemish't his stock, and had no rightfull heyres :
    Thus father, mother, brother, race, and name,
    I would have vilify'd t' advance my claime.

Report went out, and whisp'ring rumor drew
  From ev'ry quarter men of each condition
To know the sequell, whether false or true,
  To cleare their doubts, and to enforme suspition ;
And to Paule's Crosse (where state-foode, fresh and new,
  After a change, to feed their inquisition)
    The many headed beast doe flock and gather
    To heare strange tidings from their ghostly father.

There Doctor Shaw stept up : this was his theame,
  The bastard slips doe never take deepe roote ;
Who from his conduit pipe sent such a streame,
  As drench't his audience from the head to foote :
Such milke and hony, with such clouted creame,
    Flow'd from his wit, and from his tongue did shoote
      Such spleenefull venome, that all men (perplext)
      Fear'd he'd goe mad, running beside his text.

Where, having slander'd Edward's progenie,
  Taxed his lyfe, and shew'd his præcontract,
Defam'd our mother with adulterie,
  Edward nor Clarence got in lawfull act ;
Then proving me (though most preposterously)
    Yorke's true borne sonne, by us it was compact
      That I (by miracle) should come in place
      At the instant of my praise, to meet with grace.

He lookes us oft, I came not on my cue :
  At last (of course) descending to my praise,
Home it was sent ; which done, I came in view,
  And spred amongst them my abhorred rayes.
Then Shaw (verbatim) doth againe renew
    What he had spoke, things fowle need double glaze,
      Forgetting quite that twice sod meate would dull,
      Witlesse, as shamelesse, prais'd me to the full,

Which (in effect) was thus :—That I alone
  Was patterne of each princely qualitie,
For armes and vertuous disposition
  Unparalell'd ; that in forme, face, and eye,
I bore the figure and proportion
    Of Yorke, my sire : nay, to th' extremitie
      His hyred tongue my hope and glorie brings ;
      I was not borne t'obey, but rule with kings.

Which twice rub'd over, grossest flatterie,
  (Met with opinions so prejudicate)
Enforc'd the hearers universally
  To vent in murmure their concealed hate.
Another, too, (of the bald-frierie)
  Instructed on like subject to dilate,
    Grew hoarse, and in the midst (abrupt) came downe,
    Whose hyre was hate, perpetuall shame his crowne.

Such doctors were, (I doe not say there are)
  Whose breaths scall'd heaven, harts clog'd with world's desire,
That without scruple, touch of shame or feare,
  Would wrest the Scripture to make truth a lyer:
And these like mercenarie men appeare,
  That love the word for wealth, the worke for hyre;
    Whose tutor'd tongues, to take off great men's blames,
    Set stronger seales on theirs, and their owne shames.

To give more colour to this enterprise,
  My agent, Buckingham (with wit's high straines)
Prepares the citie states; men chiefly wise
  In giving way to things above their braines:
Such as were seene in measures, weights, and siz
  Of grocerie, with bread, beere, ale, and graines,
    And better knew the waight of bags and pence,
    Then matters of this weight and consequence.

These notable, wise-wealthy magistrates,
  (Such they were then, whatever they are now)
Did onely see with th' eyes of higher states;
  And what these thought (though bad) they would allow.
The sweet recorder and the cittie waytes
  Did make them sound; and ev'rie man knew how
    Better to coppie from their lookes austere,
    Then take true notes of wit from them by eare.

These gray-hayr'd sages (grave in saying little)
  My subtle Buckingham like wax had wrought,
Who surely seal'd together with the people
  He brought to tender what I long had sought ;
And, being their mouth, deliv'ring to a tittle
  Both what they would and what our selves fore-thought,
    Sollicit me (and they would have no nay)
    To take the crowne, the scepter, and the sway.

He shewes the publique good that would ensue
  The people's generall liking and applause,
Prevention of seditious plots, that grew
  Through want of execution of the lawes ;
Said, that old sores would fester and renew,
  If I tooke not the sword to right their cause.
    Behold us, then, (quoth he) with pitties eye,
    Of your accustom'd grace and clemencie.

Then I, with hart-cheekt tongue, made this reply :
  That, though I saw their heavy states with ruth,
Yet so much was my love's sinceritie
  Unto the promising hopes of Edward's youth ;
Withall, so loth to staine humilitie,
  (Professing seamelesse zeale, and naked truth)
    That I (unapt for rule and soveraigntie)
    Prefer'd content to highest monarchie.

He farther doth enforce, and I deny :
  He pleads my right, and I dissemble strong ;
Objects the princes confirm'd bastardie,
  And still the maiden's part is all my song :
At last he drives his subtill oratorie
  To shew of spleene that I their lives did wrong.
    And if, quoth he, you will not condiscend,
    We must elect some other : there's an end.

This scene, so well perform'd on either part,
    The play drew on to a catastrophe.
I added to state's double dealing art
    Devices that, by ebbing, fill'd my sea :
I hung off, to be drawne by the desert
      Of making conscience of the charge my plea,
        To take as forc'd what more then heaven I wish't,
        And to which would through troubled hel have fish't.

I still put baite on baite, to make my hooke
    The more invisible, and gave away
More then men askt : men us'd more care to looke
    Where any suite but worth the begging lay ;
Then, how to get my wing'd hand to the booke :
      Proud beggery made the whole weeke holiday ;
        For Saboths beggery was a worke of worth,
        While merit grew as banefull as the north.

Then made I civill men make ryot way,
    Men by art civill, that are ryotous ever ;
When men play arte's prize once, they fight and play,
    Such danger in the open field is never.
Art, drawne from nature, drawes her soule away,
      And then from beasts you can not men dissever,
        But in the worst part : these men, for round fees,
        Squar'd arts and all termes out by policies.

For fees I made them lawfull prove my claime,
    Disabling both my nephewes to inherit.
Gold sets up markes, hoyles, pricks for any ayme,
    That still shall hit, how wide soever merit :
Gould's chymick skill can cure an aged mayme,
      And in at death's last gaspe breath youth's first spirit ;
        Nay, so much art and nature gold controules,
        That men it makes live without manly soules.

Gold got by begging, begging not forgot,
  Could be at any hand ; bet (varied now)
For my good now they beg'd ; that theirs might not
  The font finde dry, since ever all the flow
Their sewres renewed still, and made seeth their pot.
    'Tis sacred truth : first good t'ourselves we owe.
      Thus, for themselves they supplication made,
      That I would take on me the royall trade.

I made it nice for my good, (as from theirs
  They turn'd their owne ends over all to mine)
And at the last for their good heard their prayers ;
  And as by any flood's side sinkes a pine
To take more roote, and curle his leavie hayres
  The more in bows and armes that kisse the skyne,
    So stoopt I, so to rise ; and being up,
    Both with their goods and bloods I crown'd my cup.

This fearefull doubt then being thus decided,
  As a præludium to my tragick maine,
The factious peeres now joyn'd that were divided,
  Who with all sollemne rights confirm'd my reigne.
Thus desperately I tooke the clew that guided
  Through laberinthian doubts ; and now in vaine
    That monstrous minotaure (the people) rag'd,
    Whose turbulent breath I calm'd, and fiercenes swag'd.

Now, though all heads are bare, and bend their knees,
  Yet (in themselves) my greatnes they compare
To Senecaes high-stiled tragedies,
  Embost with gold, most glorious, ritch, and faire,
Which as they ope, Thyestes greets their eyes,
  Who prov'd his children's tombe ; and then they fare
    Like men that see with horror, reade with hate :
    And so abhorred was my golden state.

For having died my hands in humane gore,
   Made black my soule, my wit a plot doth cast
To feed my ravenous appetite with more.
   My gorge was empty for a new repast;
But such a one, not ages long before
   Offer'd to time, or fame's all-sounding blast:
      Now doth my conscience play the coward's part,
      And blood, chac'd from my face, flies to my heart.

Then joy with feare, and hope with deep despaire,
   Adulterate their powers, and did engender
Confusion, horror, and blood-thirsting care,
   Which passion (mixed with distraction) render:
Now nature shrunke, and set on end my hayre,
   My hart pants thick, my pulse beates slow and tender,
      At the conception of a thought, whose hell
      Containes that torment where the divels dwell.

In shapelesse darknes I was then confin'd,
   And ev'rie thing (that erst was my delight)
Turn'd to a fiend: broad waking I was blind,
   As if enfolded in the vayle of night;
Astonishment did all my sences binde;
   Shame did appeare, dead pittie rose to light,
      When I conceav'd the murder of the princes,
      Which heav'n and hel, time, nature, death, convinces.

Yet thus my divellish spirit shooke off this trance,
   And thus my genius chid :—O, coward faint!
Did not thy wit above thy birth advance?
   Cut knotty doubts, and bars of all restraint.
Doth not thy frowne controule the frowne of chance,
   And shall thy superstitious fancy paint
      These hartlesse feares, imaginarie hell,
      And have a charme above thy politick spell!

Hast not made God a cloake to get a crowne?
  Without all shame parboyl'd thy blushlesse face?
With conquering tyranny cast pitie downe?
  Establisht wickednes, supplanted grace?
And now like to a man (ready to drowne)
  Catch at a helplesse thing? Why, this is base;
    Not like a kingly pollitician,
    But a poore ignorant plebeian.

What! wilt thou thus runne from thy selfe to error,
  And make indulgent nature now thy foe;
Plunging thy selfe into the depth of terror,
  And where once wisedome thriv'd let folly grow?
Shall ayrie vertue now become thy mirror;
  And things (meerely without) afflict thee so?
    If conscience fright, and silent shame be fear'd,
    Thou art no king, but of the popular heard.

'Tis shame (where parts agree) to make a jarre,
  To bring disturbance and distraction;
What nature hath established to marre
  Is to deface the habit she puts on:
To bring thy actions to thy conscience bar,
  So to be doom'd to swift perdition;
    But having fear'd thy conscience, seal'd thy blame,
    T'unrip the wombe againe; why, this were shame.

No, Richard: in thine owne powers still be free,
  And what seemes best thinke absolutely well:
Confirme thy strength, make good thy pollicy,
  Nor 'gainst thy name and dignity rebell.
Prove not a zelist in fond purity,
  Nor paint a heaven, nor counterfeit a hell;
    But wind into thy selfe, there set thy rest,
    So plot and execute what thou think'st best.

Maintaine thy power, diminish not thy sway,
  Nor bound thy selfe, being a boundlesse king ;
But of thy state still propagate the sea,
  And take the tribute of each petty spring :
Frame thine owne circle, and then boldly say,
  This is my center ; hether will I bring
    The lynes of all my actions, faire or foule,
    And see what power or will or can controule.

Breake ope thy black abissus, and take thence
  Worlds of advantages against the world ;
Be false and cruell still with impudence,
  And calmes with tempests on thy brow be curl'd :
From thy owne heaven derive thy influence,
  And fiend-like feare be into darknes hurl'd :
    Thy sun to sun, thy starres to starres advance,
    And let thy pompe in golden mountaines dance.

So then, (resolved) having thus debated,
  My tirannous will had laid the bloody traine,
And in my doome the princes' lives were dated,
  Whose ominous being did impeach my raigne.
I thought my selfe not absolute instated,
  Nor could make free use of my purchast gaine,
    Till without rivall I might shew my brow :
    One king in state, one sunne the heavens allow.

Now was my frostie coldnes fully thaw'd,
  And my resisted fire found open vent ;
Now I digested what so hard was chaw'd,
  And turn'd it to familiar nourishment :
Then Buckingham (my artificiall bawde,
  My hand, my factor, and my instrument)
    I grounded on to worke this last designe,
    And give the fire to this my secret myne.

Legions of divels seconded my thought
  To joyne him with me in this dangerous mayne,
Whose powrefull hand my counsell would have wrought,
  T' effect the complot of this murth'rous traine;
But here he stopt, would by no meanes be brought
  To adde this fowlenes to his former staine,
    And like on's nayles within an ulcerous sore,
    Toucht to the quick, he shrinkes, and will no more.

My motion did repeale his banisht feare,
  And feare sollicites his num'd conscience:
His coldnes mov'd my heate, which heate did beare
  The churlish temper of impatience.
And now his love from memory I teare,
  Turne his obsequious service to offence;
    For polliticians are no longer friends,
    When friends can adde no more to their mayne ends.

So did he vanish, for he now had spent
  The marrow of his trust and flatterie;
And so I us'd each servile instrument,
  When it had lost his steeled facultie:
I squeaz'd him dry, and his true service spent
  I pay'd with emptie handed usury;
    For like a pollitick well taught, full growne,
    I felt no want or fulnes but mine owne.

Besides, he had both power and subtiltie,
  And knew where I was weakest fortify'd:
Then of my selfe so much in him did lie,
  That he had got the raines to curb my pride;
Nor stood it with my kingly dignitie
  To prove his slave, that erst had been his guide.
    For his owne neck he made the fatall noose:
    They love no traytors that doe traytors use.

Great Buckingham thus pay'd with hatefull frownes,
  I chose for him the maleconted mate,
One that will kill his dearest syre for crownes,
  In hope t' advance his long dejected state :
The hope of heaven and paines of hell he drownes
    In smiles of fortune, and auspitious fate ;
      And of this ranke one Tyrrell I did frame
      To doe this deed, whose horror wants a name.

This upstart gentleman, being styl'd a knight,
  Whose back and belly had consum'd his good,
Puts forth his long-hid-head into the light,
  To crowne his valour in this act of blood :
Ages to come a catalogue may cyte
  Of such brave spirits, whose hated crests doe bud
    With homicidiall honor, and do beare
    A sable conscience in a shield of feare.

And note what state was kept when this was wrought :
  The close-stoole was my seate most eminent ;
A filthy carpet fits an ordur'd thought,
  The sences loathing, and sinne's excrement :
So Tyrrell tooke from state, whose pride had sought
  Two loathed slaves, which o'ercloy'd time did vent
    Into this sinke of shame ; in which damn'd fact
    Tyrrell commanded, and the groomes did act.

The even before the night that this was done,
  The head strong windes did rage with hydeous storme,
As red as blood discends the fearefull sunne,
  And nature had put on a dismall forme ;
Chaos was threatned by th' ecclipsed moone,
  And ravens and scrich-owles bode th' ensuing harme ;
    Then burst there forth (whiles darknes shooke hel's chaine)
    An angry comet with a smoaky traine.

The fatall howre usher'd by this ostent
  Astonisht all, and in the princes bred
Oraculous presages of th' event,
  That they like lambes were to the slaughter led :
Their spotlesse lives must cleare the element ;
  The angry comet thirsted to be fed
    With their hart bloods : they knew these stormes would cease
    When they were lodged in their graves of peace.

Thus they divin'd ; and though by zealous prayer
  They sought t' avoid the danger then so neere,
Yet such vaine hopes doe turne into despayre,
  For fate respects nor zeale, truth, love, nor feare :
Heav'ns causes knit doe never breake their square,
  But runne directly to th' effects they beare ;
    And though hard fates can never be withstood,
    Yet death confounds the bad, life crownes the good.

Thus heaven's just law, order'd by upright hand,
  They that live justly that true course do runne,
Which they that leave apparantly withstand,
  And doe pursue their owne confusion.
These innocents, being markt for angells' band,
  Keeping heaven's course as constant as the sunne,
    Although by my most bloody hand they fell,
    Yet in their fall they rose, I damn'd in hell.

These devilish slaves, whose darke deeds fly the light,
  (When sleepe in binding deawes had steep't the sences)
With glaring eyes, cloakt in the vale of night,
  Rusht in to act this murder on the princes ;
Whose horrid semblance death might well affright,
  And whose attempt even hell it selfe convinces :
    Medusa's adders in their hayre were rold,
    Not Gorgon's head more ugly to behold.

E

As they approch the bed where they repose,
  Their drumming harts panted their feare's alarms
To see the sweetnesse nature did disclose ;
  (O that such beauty should lye ope to harmes !)
There twyn'd the lilly, and the blushing rose,
  And as they claspt (like leaves) their innocent armes,
    They seemed, in the object of such glory,
    T' invite some pen to lyneate their story.

The humors and the elements combin'd
  To forme in them the abstract of perfection ;
The graces, in their sweet proportion shin'd,
  Whose radiant beames shot love, and fyr'd affection ;
And if the outward beauty from the minde,
  Receive all grace, all luster, and reflection,
    Then might one say, of eithers spirit and feature,
    Heaven held the pensill and the forme of nature.

The world's abridgement in this beauty lay,
  Thus subject to the hand of tyranny,
Whose light from darknes might have strooke the day,
  And with his beames dazled an eagles eye ;
Yet these damn'd hell hounds had the hart t'assay
  To roule these orbs up in obscuritie,
    And pash to chaos their so faire built frames,
    To sacrifice their lymbs in funerall flames.

Now, in the bed, which is the type of graves,
  And in dead sleepe, the portraicture of death,
Those dregs of men, this spawne of earth, these slaves,
  Did bury them alive, and stopt their breaths ;
Where like a sexton each himselfe behaves,
  To cover them with that which lay beneath :
    So left them sleeping in eternall rest,
    Whose sainted soules now live among the blest.

These furies now are tortur'd with despayre,
    And howle in horror of their murd'rous deede ;
They beate their brests, and teare their snaky hayre,
    In their assured torment to succeed ;
With sinfull Breaths they taint the purest ayre,
    And in their faces ev'ry one may reade,
        Guilt mixt with feares : too late they finde too well,
        That though they breath on earth they live in hell.

Now, when I saw printed in Tyrrel's brow,
    These characters of death, and shamefull gore,
I bid him study for the best meanes how
    I might requite, or he might well implore ;
But he, that did with guilt enough endowe
    His wretched state would never looke for more,
        But summing up this murder with his pride,
        He got the divell and all ; so liv'd, so dyde.

Thus without feare, arm'd with Herculean force,
    I saw this hell, my thoughts had shapt and bred :
If fearefull Hydra had opposed my course,
    I should have left the monster never a head ;
Or like Roomes tyrant, with as small remorse,
    Thousand contracted lives have butchered,
        To raise my glorie to this compleate frame,
        And set my foote upon the throate of shame.

Yet, now my life was conversant with danger,
    Feare and suspition did perturb my sleepe.
Th' apparent hate of men stir'd up my anger,
    And charged pistols for defence I keepe :
For since I had profest my selfe a stranger
    To every good, in blood and sinne so deepe,
        My sores were to be rub'd t'avoide their harmes :
        Whom guilt sollicits, circumspection armes.

They that no ill commit, no ill need feare,
  And truth is their best armor of defence :
Ill comes not when before it was not there,
  And weapons fit a wounded conscience.
Tyrants the privie coate had need to weare,
  And ever waking keep their troubled sence ;
    So kept I watch, and stood upon my guard,
    My steele still drawne, of mine own shadow fear'd.

Now the Lancastrian line, that scarce was seene,
  With sword, insted of pen, begins to raze
The line of Yorke, whose inke is blackest spleene,
  To blot my glorie, and my name deface.
The frost-bit rose now sprouts and waxeth greene,
  Wanting but time to spread with wonted grace :
    The white rose must be joined with the red,
    To propagate faire stems in one chast bed.

Richmond my brother's daughter to espouse,
  The sweet Elizabeth, is mark't by fate,
Which to prevent my lyon spirit I rouze,
  With that faire lyonesse t' incorporate ;
Which though nor lawes of God nor man allowes,
  Yet to establish and secure my state,
    I sought with wilfull lust and powerfull awe,
    To crosse the banes and over-rule the law.   .

First Buckingham, whose hopes were vainely fed
  To breake the ice for Richmond with his powre,
I march't against, and by good fortune sped ;
  My starres herein did smile, and his did lowre.
I prick't him kindly, he as kindly bled
  His ancient love, and so in happy howre,
    I pai'd th' arrerages of his lent good,
    And had m' acquittance sealed with his blood.

O, Buckingham ! thou wert too open brested
  And spent'st too freely to receive thy right ;
For of my state by thee I was invested,
  A debt farre greater then I could requite.
Some states-men's hands are shut, their bounty chested,
  And ill doe they abide those men in sight,
    That may upbrayde with unrequited good :
    Such bonds are seldome cancell'd, but with blood.

Next Anne, my wife, whose being did deny
  My match with my fayre neece Elizabeth,
Fell sodaine sicke with griefe or jealousie ;
  And all my love would not preserve her breath.
I gave her medicines for sterilitie
  And she grew fruitfull in the bed of death,
    Her issue crawling wormes ; and there she lyes,
    Whose love, and life, loe ! thus I memorize.

This was that creature that I woo'd and wonn,
  Over her bleeding husband stab'd by me :
Such different persons never saw the sunne,
  He, for perfection, I, deformitie.
She wept and smil'd, hated and lov'd in one,
  Such was her vertue, my hypocrisie :
    Thus women's griefes, nor loves, are dyde in graine,
    For either's colour time or men can staine.

For farther proofe my sister queene I chose,
  Professing truth to her, t' her daughter, love ;
Insinuating with such artfull gloze,
  As if the god of eloquence should move ;
And notwithstanding all the banefull woes
  She had sustain'd by me, I made her prove
    My loves attourney, furthering my sute
    T'astonish wonder, and strike rumor mute.

By this I instance how these fooles are caught.
  With honors baites, or tickled with their praise ;
Whose flexible conditions may be wrought
  To any forme, subjects for sports and playes :
Angels they seeme, and are with angels bought,
  Guilded corruption, nature's falsed glaze ;
    No meane in their affects, in passion moving,
    No moment in their teares, nor faith in loving.

Inconstant sex ! no sooner full then wayning,
  In weakenes dying, and imperfect borne ;
Their scanted wils, like halfe fac't moones, complaining,
  Which to supply they make the forked horne :
Nor hot, nor cold ; now loving, then disdaining,
  The fautors of deceipt, of truth the scorne ;
    Like cotton buds, which none can bruise or pull,
    But being put forth, like them they turne to wooll.

Such were my wyles, I could deceive deceite,
  Guild imperfections with imperfect glorie,
Building on ruines my uncertaine state,
  Laugh at oppression from prides promontorie.
I sooth'd my pompe with an eternall date,
  And in ambition perfected my storie ;
    Which word let fame to after ages sound,
    As of my life the pyramed and ground.

And thus with hartie nerves and spirit undaunted,
  I plow'd up graves, and sow'd my seede in blood,
And in my crop of honors proudly vaunted,
  Feeding my thoughts with momentarie good ;   .
And though my state on brittle sand was planted,
  Yet fear'd not I death's all-subverting flood :
    Of elementall stuffe I thought the mind,
    Vertue but ayre, and all religion winde.

FINIS.

THE

TRAGEDIE OF RICHARD THE THIRD.

Now, whiles my lawlesse love was set on foote,
   Entended as a barre to Richmond's claime,
Thinking to put mine axe unto the roote,
   To cross his hopes with unrecover'd maime,
Revenge look't big, and heaven began to shoote
     Warre's fierie darts ; and now my glorie's frame
       (Founded on wrong, and rais'd in blood and teares)
       Begins to shake and fall about mine eares.

O thou which bred'st all mischiefe in my brest,
   And mad'st me swell with unasswag'd desire ;
Thou vast conceiving chaos indigest,
   Thou toplesse builder of great Babel's spyre ;
(Damned ambition) thou that did'st infest,
   And set my nature on a quenchlesse fire,
     Now (prest with thy huge weight) too late I finde
     There is no hell to an aspiring minde.

And as the taper play'd within the night,
   Where men doe firmely sit, or walke, or stand,
Raiseth their shadowes to the places' hight,
   Then to the ground in turning of a hand ;
Now it empaires them by the waving light,
   And then extends their lengths themselves beyond ;
     So fortune playes with kings and worldly states,
     She tosses, turnes, reares, and precipitates.

As one that drinkes more then he can containe,
 He surfets in excesse, and duls his tast;
And then (the fume spred through his poares and braine)
 He speakes his secret'st thoughts, and seemes disgrast,
Nor doth desist, till in his drunken vaine
 His intellectuall powres are so defact,
  That (loosing th' office of his feete) he lyes
  Shamefull and naked to all sober eyes:

So I, in thirst of glorie, rule, and state,
 Drinking excessively, and past my fill,
Swinging in lust and thoughts intemperate,
 Drunke in ambition and my sensuall will,
Was so transparent in my latest date,
 And all my good so swallow'd in my ill,
  That in my staggering pride, and shamefull fall,
  I grew a monster and a scorne to all.

I, that once thought that no man could be blest
 In moderate kinde of humane blessednes,
And in my tyrannous licence did suggest
 To comprehend (in pompe) all happines;
Gave reignes to lust, and in my will supprest
 The rule of reason, (man's sole sovereignesse)
  That to the world's doome still prefer'd mine owne,
  And pitcht my hopes no lower then a crowne:

I, that did make no conscience to plot,
 And perpetrate all beastiall cruelty;
That harrow'd earth and hell for what I got,
 As if those tipes would last eternally;
In goodnes cold, in mischiefe ever hot,
 And in my damned tracts of pollicie
  Had sowne men's harts, and with unfeeling taints
  Did dye my hands in innocent blood of saints:

I, that could taint soules with corrupting breath,
  And from their brests roote faith and pietie,
Steeling their spirits for acts of closest death,
  And suck the hart of their abilitie,
Then raise fresh bloods, and set the dry beneath,
  Fester'd in conscience of their villany,
    Then rack them with delayes, reward with ayre,
    And laugh to see them perish in despaire :

I, that at best held vertue and religion
  No other things but well mixt elements,
Nor vice nor ill but humor's disposition
  Depraved by the bodie's instruments ;
Esteem'd the soule subject to death's corruption ;
  Nor thought all these but naturall events,
    And their disorder cur'd by phisick's skill,
    And nothing subject to th' Eternall will :

Now did my conscience, that lay smothered
  Under this pile of damn'd impietie,
And seem'd (as with greene fuell maistered)
  Conceall'd and prison'd in obscuritie,
Shew'd that by sin 'twas rather comforted
  Then any way depriv'd of facultie,
    And in their flame did rage so much the more
    By how much it did seeme restrain'd before.

Now all my acts of murder, sinne, and shame,
  (Bred by ambition and my tyrannous will)
Appear'd upon my head like Ætna's flame,
  Or like a beacon fyr'd upon a hill :
Now rumor gives the eccho to my fame ;
  Uprores and insurrections 'gin to fill
    All places vast ; and now in feare I start,
    To fall beneath the mountaine of my hart.

O˙ how I curst my aspick flatterie
　　That shed such venome in my rationall powre,
I curst the glasse that so corruptedly
　　Did shew the face of vice to smile, not lowre:
Now for each priviledg'd mischiefe did I lye
　　A butt to torment; and a fearefull showre,
　　　　(By the black vapor of my sin being bred)
　　　　With blood and vengeance swolne, hung o're my head.

Thus in the wayning splendor of my pride,
　　Compast with danger, and assaylde with feares,
And in my thoughts all torments multiply'd
　　That might augment the burthen of my cares,
I found myselfe so weakely fortifyde
　　Against the powerfull battery of despaires,
　　　　That I was plung'd into hel's deepe abisse,
　　　　Secluded from all comfort, joy, or blisse.

Nor did the ancient poets idely faine
　　Erinnis and the damn'd Eumenides,
Since even those furies in their maske containe
　　The morall of my tortur'd tyranies:
For th' apparitions of ensuing paine
　　So danted me with their extremities,
　　　　That I was rackt in terror of my doome,
　　　　And made that present which was but to come.

Then dreadfull melancholly did convert
　　My nature to the temper of my braine,
Which, soaked with my spleene, disturb'd my heart,
　　And through my body spred a pois'nous bane:
It did confound my sense and ev'ry part,
　　Each muscle, sinnew, artire, joint, and vaine,
　　　　Had lost their naturall working, and prepare
　　　　To set me in the high-way to despaire.

Such was the horror of my malady,
  Distract with feare of that I was t' inherit,
That it corrupted every facultie,
  Congeal'd my blood, and dull'd my active spirit ;
Thus my whole nature felt like sympathy
    With my despairefull soule for sinfull merit,
      For all the functions of my soule and sence
      Were maymed by my wounded conscience.

My reason dotes ; my soule did idle sit,
  Wanting fit matter of intelligence ;
Organs deprav'd, and stupifyde my wit,
  My understanding weake, unsound my sence,
And every part disabled, and unfit
    To comfort or relieve my conscience :
      Hopelesse and helplesse all my powers agree
      In desperation's gulph to swallow me.

And as we see the eye, the eare, or sent,
  Affected long, and over vehemently,
Retaine their species in the instrument,
  Though absent be the moving qualitie ;
So the internall sences, strongly bent
    To fearefull objects of obscuritie,
      To judge of things by their depraved kinde,
      Give passion vigor, and make reason blind.

The sunne, the moone, and planets of my nature,
  So fearefully ecclipsed in their light ;
My inward darknes casting on my feature
  A semblance ghastly pale, and full of fright ;
My leprous soule deformed as my stature,
    Did in these tragick terrors seeme t' excite
      The thoughtfull presage of my destinie,
      To be accomplisht in my tragedie.

Likewise my name enter'd in hel's black roule,
 So infinite my actions of arrest,
My grim-fac't conscience ceazing on my soule,
 And my tormentor ever in my breast:
So not the minde alone, but body whole,
  Equally feeling, and alike distrest,
   Such watch they kept, such clamor they did make,
   That waking I did dreame, and sleeping wake.

Such was my passion, of all faith bereav'd
 Which should apply a salve unto my wound,
That in my minde hell onely was conceav'd,
 Which did all thought and hope of heaven confound:
Thus my despairefull melancholly weav'd
  The web of my affliction, and I found
   My state so desperate, and my sin so great,
   That no repentant meanes could expiate.

Should I have fill'd the ayre with plaints and cries,
 Have wrung my hands in griefe, strayn'd blood in feares ;
Eate into marble with my still bent knees,
 And all the center rotted with my teares ;
Such was the clamor of my villanies,
  And so importunate were my despaires,
   That nothing (as I thought) would satisfie
   Th' offended justice of the Deitie.

The setled center easier might assume
 The heavenly motion, that turnes ever round ;
Huge whales might sooner fly with feathered plume,
 And birds, like wormes, creepe on the base ground,
Ere I could hope, or ever might presume,
  By my repentance mercy to have found ;
   For, prest with sin, and of all grace bereaven,
   I could not lift one thought so high as heaven.

Not Saul, that (being possest) dyde reprobate,
   Not Esau's selfe, that did his birth-right sell ;
Not Judas, mark't for veng'ance by his fate,
   Not those which were devoured quick to hell ;
Not hardned Pharao, all as desperate,
    Nor cursed and forlorne Achitophel,
      Could be more surely seall'd in Heaven's just doome,
      Then I in conscience for the wrath to come.

Thus blasted with the whirlewind of God's breath,
   And shaken with the terror of his wrath,
Veng'ance above me, and hell-fire beneath,
   So void of grace, and so exempt from faith,
What could I looke for but eternall death,
    Since all my life was progrest in that path ?
      Now did I fondly wish, in my despayre,
      To be resolv'd to th' element of ayre.

When drowsie Morpheus with his mace addrest
   My turbulent spirits to a quiet truce,
My thoughts scarce gave me sleepe, that sleepe no rest ;
   Though bound my sences, yet my sinne was loose ;
For th' images of outward things (imprest
    In common sence) did (as it is their use)
      Present unto my waking phantasie
      The horrid visions of my tyrannie.

For my domestick feares (that wholy tend
   To extacies and broken sleepes unsound)
Did to my brayne black fumes of horror send,
   Rais'd from dispare and melancholies ground ;
Whereon the phantasie did apprehend,
    And forge such terrible objects, that I found
      My selfe oft strangled through those dreames of terror,
      Which shew'd my death, and hell, as through a mirror.

Such apparitions frighted me in sleepe,
  My conscience unappeas'd, my sinne still crying;
These terrible impressions were so deepe,
  That, waking, I was transt, and living, dying:
I wish't I had beene made a worme, to creepe,
  Or from a worthlesse egge beene hatch't from flying;
    Or, like proude Nabuchadnezar, to nourish
    My beastiall nature, and like beasts to perrish.

Thus sinne a venom'd tooth from hell did borrow,
  Which ranckled to the death with deadly byte;
I sorrow'd desperatly, because my sorrow
  Was all too late to helpe my helplesse plight:
I plow'd uppon my barren heart, whose furrow
  (Not deaw'd with teares, nor sowne with seedes contrite)
    Could yeeld no frute, but ranckned with sinns ayre,
    For hopeful faith brought thornes of sharp despaire.

Damnation's feare did make me penitent,
  Which reprobates may have with God's elect;
But fayth and grace (whose ends are to repent)
  Were farre remov'd, and absent in effect:
I knew my sinne with sorrowes languishment,
  In conscience sincking, and in horror wrak't,
    But that repentance, which should save and raise me,
    Justice forbids me, and despaire denaies me.

Now England's genius doth begin to swell,
  Whose spirit, long supprest, breakes out in fyre;
The peeres doe stirr, the commons doe rebell,
  Gyrles great with spleene, and women sharpe with ire,
Old men takes armes, children (new crept from shell)
  Wrong and oppression doe with rage inspire:
    Factions now rend the state in severall parts,
    Swords in their hands, and vengeance in their hearts.

Richmond hath set his foote upon my strand,
  Who out of many letts hath wrought his course,
And like a streame, which lower banckes withstand,
  Swells o're his bounds, and spreeds his flowing sourse:
The wrong incensed peerés augment his band,
  And give his weakenes a resistfull force.
        Of those that did my tyrannous yoake still beare,
        None lent their strengths in love, but all in feare.

Who in their staggering doubts of warres event,
  And to secure their howses from attaint,
Did set a coulor on their forst entent,
  And with could faiths relieved my hope as faint;
Distracted were their mindes, their hearts were rent:
  Weake are the powers that fight upon constraint.
        Of some I tooke firme hostage, to assure them,
        And promis'd others mountaines, to procure them.

From the could north (summon'd by my commaund)
  I had a company of frozen hearts,
Who seem'd the very scar-crowes of the land,
  So poore they were; ill furnisht at all parts:
These halfe fac't starvelings, and this bandles band,
  These ragged outsides, and these tattered shirts,
        Came as to warme them nere the western light,
        With mawes to feede, rather than hearts to fight.

These were the souldiers that I kept in pay,
  Such fayntlings never yet were prest with coyne;
Whose heavy lookes their duller spirits betray:
  To make hope falter in my warres designe,
All sought to loose rather then win the day,
  And seem'd more Richmond's part then friends of myne:
        Yet these I term'd true hearts, with falsed stile,
        And hartned them with many a hartles smile.

And, though environ'd with a darksome feare,
    Yet in my face I forst a seeming light,
Whose substance crude, and could, I did out weare
    The day in cares, in waking howers the night :
Unsetled were my motions, and did beare
    Undoubted semblance of distracted plight.
      My conscience prick't, soliciting my mynd
      With blood, for my most bloody deedes assign'd.

O how I band the Welch with bitter spite,
    Ap Thomas, Griffeth, Herbert, and their traine,
That with poore Richmond's handfull joyn'd their might,
    To take part with the meane, and leave the mayne :
But when they swore to our defensive right,
    With sence reserv'd they kept their names from stayne ;
      For I usurpt, and had noe right at all ;
      Their guardian angells prompt their rize, my fall.

Yet on I must with these my dangerous friends,
    To try the chance of vengeance threatning warrs,
Where guilt gives terror, terror mischiefe lends,
    And mixe their malice with my fatall starres :
The devlish fury in my brest entends,
    In spite of danger and all opposite barrs ;
      To cut this knot the mistick fates conteyne,
      And set my life and kingdome on this mayne.

Richmond comes on, reliev'd with still supplies,
    Whose firmest faiths give hart to his just ayme,
Steeling the back of his great enterprize
    With Cambro-Brittaines, men of taintlesse name :
My strength is trustles, his in true harts lyes,
    And still encreaseth going, like to fame ;
      Angels attend him with their imminent powre,
      Auspicious are his starres, and mine doe lowre.

The prayers of old men, and the nerves of young,
  Give vigor to his arme, and prompt his spirit :
Curses and rage (through tyrany and wrong)
  Attend my action and my hatefull merit :
I faint in millions, he in hundreds strong ;
    For not the oddes of multitudes inherit
      The victor's prize, since warre (in heaven's just lawes)
      Is ever sway'd by justice of the cause.

Warr 's the tribunall where all deeds of armes
  Receive their equall and their partlesse doome ;
Not fortune's spels, nor legions with their charmes,
  But must give fate preeminence and roome,
Though men, like gyants, with their proud alarms,
    Doe brave the heav'ns ; yet if Jove's thunder come
      In awful veng'ance downe, such pride he quailes ;
      So not presumption, then, but truth prevailes.

The bloody field is pitcht, survey'd the ground ;
  The centynels are plac't ; perdu's are sent,
Souldiers entrenched and encamped round,
  And in the midst advanc'd my shining tent ;
Counsels assembled for directions sound ;
    Advantages propos'd for detriment :
      All things dispos'd, night comes, strong watch wee keep,
      When weighty cares doe summon me to sleepe.

Now doth my conscience agitate my feares
  In visions of my waking phantasie ;
Now each particular action appeares
  A strong appealant of my tyrany :
Murder sounds horror in my deafned eares,
    And all my deeds of damn'd impietie
      Presse to the barr where I receive my doome
      Of death-stabs heere, and infinite to come.

F

Me thought I saw in those affrighting dreames
  My slaughtred numbers round about my bed,
Op'ning their wounded mouthes in crimson streames,
  And powring blood upon my tyrannous head:
The furies' brands (me thought) shed flaming beames,
  To wast me in my passage through the dead,
    Where, at hel's mouth, each howling spirit proclaimes,
    And rings my welcome with their clamorous chaines.

Me thought I saw and heard the loathsome plight
  Of dying men, how bound in frosts they lye,
Swimming in cold sweates, and bereft of light,
  Their entrailes gnawne, pulse stay'd, and veines drawne dry,
Their ratling throats, fur'd tongues, their broken sight;
  Their gasping breaths, their lookes deformitie,
    Their earthy savor in expiring breath.
    O, horrid dreame! but O, more fearefull death!

Me thought, likewise, the dismall rav'ns did croke
  As I approch't my death to passe the graves;
The earth did shake, and conjur'd tempests broke
  In hydeous noises from their bellowing caves,
Which threw downe turrets, root the stoutest oake:
  Then from the clouds the arme of vengeance waves,
    And gives the signall to the bloody fight,
    Where thousand swords divide me and the light.

These violent distractions broke in sunder
  The heavy band that bound my sences fast,
Whose frightfull visions made me wild with wonder;
  Yet up I rose: then had I slept my last,
And whiles with ghastly visage I did ponder,
  Present, ensuing, and the times long past,
    I started from my trance with ragefull teene,
    Taking a dragon's spirit, a tyger's spleene.

And as the motions of all naturall things
   Prove swiftest in their ends, more strong enclin'd,
As torrents roare, deriv'd from smallest springs,
   And gentle blasts doe turne to boystrous winde ;
So I resolv'd to put on fierie wings,
   And in my end adde spirit to my minde,
     For yeelding thoughts besit the basest slaves ;
     Kings should soare high, although they drop to graves.

The morning's chanticlere proclaim'd the day,
   Whose lowring countenance vail'd the God of light ;
Yet glistring armor (spite of morning's gray)
   To valiant mindes do yeeld a cheereful sight :
The roll'd up ensigne, when it doth display,
   Gives hart and coulor to the martiall wight :
     From Richmond's armes his harts took such bright shine,
     But leaden spirits could take no life from mine.

Now was my battell rang'd on Bosworth plaine,
   The vantgard order'd, and the wings were set :
Norfolke, (my chieftaine) with much sweat and paine,
   Temper'd my frozen harts with his kind heate :
Surrey and he bore mindes that had no staine,
   Both well approv'd in armes and martiall feate.
     Our standards both advanc't in open sight,
     Summons are given to prepare the fight.

My men with souldior's rethorick I excite,
   Enforce the vildnes of mine enemie.
Th' injustice of his cause, of ours the right ;
   Our wealthy states, their desperate povertie,
Their fainting force, and our assured might ;
   Our living honors, and their infamy :
     So I concluded with these hartning words,
     St. George for England, and for me their swords.

Now rotten sin gives ripenes to my fate,
　And Jove doth vaile the curtaine of the sky,
Reflecting beames of favor and sterne hate
　On Richmond's conquest and my tragedie :
Heaven's singing motion (that devoures live's date,
　　The working organs of the deitie)
　　　　Hastes to my period, when I must be throwne
　　　　From height of pride to depth of Acheron.

Signall is given, and the sound of death,
　Showts, drums, and trumpets deafen all our eares ;
Brests buts for shafts, and swords in flesh doe sheath ;
　Horse meet with horse, and speares are lin'd with speares ;
Blood blends with blood, and breath doth mix with breath ;
　Life flies with life, and beeres are laid by beeres ;
　　Mazors to bils doe stand for butchers' blocks,
　　Fire twin'd with lightning, thunder join'd with shocks.

Bellona rag'd not so as I did storme :
　My lyon spirit hunts Richmond for my pray.
I out-fac't death in his most ugly forme,
　And through the thickest shocks I hew'd my way ;
My spirit was like whirle-winde, and mine arme
　A pointed comet in this cruell fray,
　　Streaming forth blood, and foming rage and gall :
　　Deathfull my spleene, my fury funerall.

Unequall'd was my more then mortall ire :
　Hel's ever burning lymbeck did distill
The spirit of divels in my quenchlesse fire,
　Wishing such power to damne as hart to kill.
My winged horse did pegase my desire ;
　Windes in my passion, th' ocean in my will,
　　My cloud-congested rage dissolv'd like thunder ;
　　My valour more prodigious then wonder.

But soone my archers slack their strongest bent,
  My souldiers' steele rebated ; yet (more keene)
They brandish malice with one free consent,
  And against me convert their pointed spleene.
Stanley with Richmond joines his regiment ;
    Some fled, some stood at gaze, the rest were seene
      With idle action to maintaine the field :
      Powre faintly answer'd argues will to yeeld.

Then, as I had attain'd the wished ken
  Of Richmond's selfe by noted markes he wore,
In bloudy sweate I spur'd through slaughtred men,
  To quench my fierie spirit with his gore.
Brandon (his valiant standard-bearer then)
    I slew, with stout opposers many more ;
      And with spent blood being weake in ev'ry part,
      I fail'd to set my seale on Richmond's heart.

My horse being slaine, with him I fell to ground,
  And yet even then was not disanimate,
For my high spirit above my flesh did bound,
  Scorning the limit of my mortall date ;
Till with their thickest troopes enclosed round,
  And wrastling manly with malignant fate,
      They character'd in wounds my tyrannie,
      And thus perform'd my bloody tragedie.

My braine they dasht, which flew on ev'ry side,
  As they would shew my tracts of policie :
My yeares with stabs, my dayes they multiplide
  In drops of blood, t' expresse my crueltie :
They pierst my hart, evaporating pride,
  And mangled me like an anatomie,
      And then with horses drag'd me to my tombe.
      Thus finish't I my fate by heaven's just doome.

Yee that, in stately madnesse of desire,
　　Doe thinke your selves firme center'd in your spheres ;
Yee that (subjecting sence) like gods aspire,
　　In rising hopes confounding headlong feares,
Behold in me your suddaine quenched fire,
　　To depth of hell falne from those lofty stayres :
　　　　Asswage your thirst betimes, remit your height,
　　　　For if yee fall y' are crush't with your owne weight.

But if ye slight my counsell, still feed lust,
　　Pamper proud flesh, drinke sinfull Lethæ free,
Till tyme and death resolve your trunkes to dust,
　　Your soules to torments, names to infamy.
And so farewell, for back againe I must
　　Unto the horrid shades of destiny :
　　　　Now doe I sinke, as erst in pride I fell,
　　　　And to leave fame on earth thus div'd to hell.

Now England's chaos was reduc't to order
　　By god-like Richmond, whose successive stems
The hand of time hath branch't, in curious border,
　　Unto the mem'rie of thrice royall James :
An angel's trumpe be his true fame's recorder,
　　And may that Brittaine Phœbus from his beames,
　　　　In glorie's light his influence extend,
　　　　His offspring countles ; peace, nor date, nor end.

Hæc decies repetita placebit.

FINIS.

NOTES.

Page 3, line 8. Since commonly the world's *obsequious* insinuations in trifles prove their obsequies of no more importance.] Shakespeare constantly uses " obsequious" in the sense of *funereal*, or at the obsequies of the dead. See Shakespeare, edit. published by Whittaker and Co., v. 270, 352 ; vii. 206 ; viii. 490.

Page 4, line 15. I know your true *noblesse* out of the common way.] So Shakespeare, " Richard II.," act iv., sc. 1, uses " nobless" for nobleness, according to the 4to, 1597, and as the verse requires ; though later old impressions, and all modern editions, injuriously substitute *nobleness*.

> " Would God, that any in this noble presence
> Were enough noble to be upright judge
> Of noble Richard : then, true *nobless* would
> Learn him forbearance from so foul a wrong."

Page 6, line 6. As hee is *ingenious* or *ingenuous*.] Shakespeare sometimes uses these two words indifferently. See edit. Whittaker and Co., ii., 294 ; vi., 535.

Page 6, line 22. I set up my rest.] A phrase originally from gunnery, of the commonest occurrence : it was also used figuratively at primero, and, perhaps, at some other games of cards. See Shakespeare, edit. Whittaker and Co., ii., 155 ; vi., 474, 489.

Page 7, line 13. Will sell like good old *Gascoine*.] Chapman here seems to intend a play upon the word " Gascoine," as the name of a wine, and as the name of our old English poet, George Gas-

coigne, who died in 1577, and whose poetical works were collected
and published about 1572, and still more completely in 1587, 4to.

Page 8, line 17. *Fore-speake* the sale of thy sound poesie.] To
" forespeak" was of old not unfrequently used for to *forbid.* So in
" Antony and Cleopatra," act iii., sc. vii. Cleopatra tells Antony,

> " Thou hast forspoke my being in these wars,
> And say'st, it is not fit."

Page 8, line 26. ————————— who then a rounde

> On oaten pipe no further boasts his skill.]

Referring to the rustic character in which the writer of these lines
had printed his " Britannia's Pastorals," which he dated from the
Inner Temple (not a very rural vicinity), June 18, 1613.

Page 11, line 4. Your Pasquil like a mad-cap runs away.] Nicholas
Breton was the author of a tract, printed in 1600, called " Pasquil's
Mad-cap," &c., but in this line Daborne (the dramatist of whom
so much is said in " The Alleyn Papers," and who afterwards went
into the church, and had a living in Ireland), seems to use Pasquil
merely in the sense of a lampoon, and to have had no particular
reference.

Page 11, line 18. To his friend the author upon his Richard.] It
is to be borne in mind, as stated in the introduction, that, in 1602,
Ben Jonson was engaged in writing a historical drama for Hens-
lowe's company, called "Richard Crook-back." See Shakespeare,
edit. Whittaker and Co., v., 345. Shakespeare's " Richard the
Third," at that date, had been, perhaps, eight years on the stage.

Page 13, line 5. What magick, or what *fiend's* infernall hand,

> Reares my tormented ghost from *Orcus* flame.]

As a specimen of typography, in the age of Shakespeare, this poem
begins very unpropitiously with two gross misprints in the two first
lines, which run in the original,

> " What magick, or what *friend's* infernall hand,
> Reares my tormented ghost from *Oreus* flame."

We have, of course, corrected such errors, but not without due
notice.

Page 13, line 14. When all their veniall and petty crimes

> Are *expiate*, but mine will never cease].

C. B. here seems to use " expiate" in the sense in which it is twice employed by Shakespeare, viz. *expired*, or *at an end*. The first instance occurs in his " Richard III.," act iii., sc. 3.

<blockquote>" Make haste: the hour of death is *expiate*."</blockquote>

The other instance is found in his twenty-second sonnet. This use of the word was not peculiar to Shakespeare.

Page 13, line 16. —— all worlds and *times*.] The old copy reads *time* for " times."

Page 14, line 10. Whose percell guylt my *touch* will not endure.] Shakespeare uses " touch " just in the same sense in " Richard III.," act iv., sc. 2.

<blockquote>" Ah, Buckingham ! now do I play the *touch*,
   To try if thou be current gold indeed,"</blockquote>

or only " percell guylt," or *partly gilt*, and not true gold.

Page 14, line 14. How wanton Salmasis, with lust impure,
<blockquote>Cleaves to your soules !]</blockquote>

The poem imputed (perhaps falsely) to Francis Beaumont, under the title of " Salmasis and Hermaphroditus," had been printed in 1602, 4to. See Shakspeare, edit. Whittaker and Co., i. p. cxvi, note 3.

Page 15, line 13. My tongue in firie dragons spleene I steepe.] In " Richard III.," act v., sc. 3, Shakespeare uses the expression, " inspire us with the spleen of fiery dragons."

Page 16, line 22. The characters of spleen and virulent *deeds*.] The rhyme would shew that we ought to read *deed* for " deeds," but poets of old were not always particular in this respect.

Page 17, line 1. And as a raven's beake, pointed to south,
<blockquote>Crokes following ill.]</blockquote>

This passage illustrates two lines in Ben Jonson's " Masque of Queens," represented in Feb. 1609-10.

<blockquote>" As soon as she turn'd her beak to the south,
   I snatch'd this morsel out of her mouth."</blockquote>

Upon which the author's own comment is the following :—" As if that piece were sweeter, which the wolf had bitten, or the raven picked and more effectuous : and to do it at her turning to the south, as with the prediction of a storm ; which, though they be but minutes in ceremony, being observed, make the act more dark and full of horror." This Masque is about to be printed by the Shakespeare Society from the author's own MS., preserved in the British

Museum, with the existence of which no editor of Ben Jonson's works was acquainted.

Page 23, line 26. How they dispatched suters that implored them.] We may suspect, from the corresponding rhymes of "adore them" and "bore them," that we ought to read this line.

"How they dispatched suters that *implore* them."

It might not, however, be a misprint, as poets of that day were not exact in their rhymes. See note on page 16, line 22.

Page 24, line 23. The sunne exhaled steames.] Of course "sunne exhaled" is here a compound epithet, and ought to have been printed *sunne-exhaled.*

Page 25, line 32. Therefore I thought to be myself alone.] Compare "Henry VI.," pt. 3, act v., sc. 6, "I am myself alone," &c. Several preceding passages, which it was needless to note, will have reminded the reader of Shakespeare.

Page 26, line 1.] And as your-selfe lov'd politicks n'ere care.] The old printer obviously did not understand this line, or he would have given it thus:

"And as your *selfe-lov'd* politicks n'ere care."

"Self-loved" for *self loving;* the passive for the active participle, very common in Shakspeare, and writers of the time.

Page 26, line 7. *I forst* no publique wrack.] That is, *I heeded not,* or *cared not for* any public wrack. The expression was not unusual: see Shakespeare, edit. Whittaker and Co., ii., 367; viii., 444, &c.

Page 27, line 3. To him that impt my fame with Clio's quill.] A clear allusion to Shakespeare, and to his play on the history of Richard III. is contained in this and the following stanza. See Shakespeare, edit. Whittaker and Co., i., ccxlvi.

Page 27, line 17. Nor wits nor chronicles.] We may more than suspect a misprint here, and that we ought to read "Nor *acts*, nor chronicles," alluding to the acts of a drama, as distinguished from a chronicle: in old writing it would be easy for a cursory eye to misread *acts* "wits."

Page 27, line 23. There is a fate your boundles hope *convinces.*] Nothing was much more usual, in the time of Shakespeare, than to use the verb "to convince" in the etymological sense of to *overcome* or *conquer.* See also p. 34.

Page 28, line 7. —— and hell sulpher spew'd.] This passage is thus misprinted in the old copy, *a hell sulpher and 'spew'd*: there can be little doubt that we have restored the right reading, which is at least intelligible.

Page 29, line 7. A murder that might make the *starres* to wink.] In the original, the letter *t* has dropped out in the word " starres."

Page 29, line 10. The *dy* being bar'd.] The original has " The *by* being bar'd;" but the context seems to shew that we should read " the *dy* (or *die*) being *barr'd*:" to bar a die was a phrase among gamblers.

Page 30, line 7. And, being not shap't for love.] Here the author clearly had the opening soliloquy of " Richard III." in his mind, especially the line—

  " But I, that am not shap'd for sportive tricks," &c.

Page 33, line 9. Truth had a *tattering* stand.] Or, as we now spell it, *tottering*: on the other hand, the word which we now spell *tattered* was of old often printed *tottered*, of which many examples might be produced in the time of Shakespeare.

Page 33, line 19. My counsell's consistory.] This is precisely the phrase that Richard, in Shakespeare's tragedy, applies to Buckingham:

  " My other self, *my counsel's consistory*."

Richard III., act ii., sc. 2.

Page 35, line 20. Which neither bounds *contain'd*.] So the original copy, and it may be right; but the present tense, as in the conclusion of the line, would seem preferable.

Page 36, line 4. *Spred* gloomy darkness.] In the old copy "spred " (spread) is misprinted *sped*.

Page 37, line 7. In jealousy had *Argus* hundred eyes.] " *Argoes* hundred eyes," in the old copy.

Page 37, line 21. But now her fame by a vile play doth grow.] Alluding to a drama upon the story of Jane Shore, of which there were several of old. One of them is mentioned with Shakespeare's " Pericles," in a tract called " Pymlico, or Run Red-cap," printed in 1609. See the Introduction. A play called " Shore's Wife," by H. Chettle and John Day, is mentioned by Henslowe in his

Diary in 1603. In Thomas Heywood's "Edward VI.," a play in two parts recently printed for this Society, Jane Shore is a prominent character.

Page 39, line 17. I came not on my *cue*.] i. e., at the proper moment—an expression derived from the stage, the "cue" denoting the *tail*, or end, of the speech of one character, where another takes up the dialogue. The fact is historical: Sir T. More, in his "Life and Reign of Edward V.," has this passage. "At these words, 'twas designed the Protector should have entered, as if it had been by chance; and the conspirators hoped that the multitude, taking the doctor's words as coming from the immediate inspiration of the Holy Ghost, would have been induced to have cried out ' God save King Richard!' Which artifice was prevented, either by the doctor's making too much haste to come to that part of his sermon, or the Lord Protector's negligence to come in at the instant when he was saying it, for it was over before he came, and the priest was entered on some other matter when the Duke appeared."

Page 40, line 29. The sweet recorder and the cittie waytes
    Did make them sound.]
A play upon the word "recorder," meaning the chief law authority of the city and a musical instrument, here seems obvious. "The city waits" were the nocturnal musicians of London: in Beaumont and Fletcher's "Knight of the Burning Pestle," "the waits of Southwark" are mentioned.

Page 41, line 32. We must elect some other: there's an end.] We may notice here a curious and characteristic variance between the folio edition of "Richard III." in 1623, and the older quartos: in the latter, at the end of his speech to the king, Buckingham, according to the folio, exclaims,

   " Come citizens; we will entreat no more:"
but in the quartos it stands thus:

   " Come citizens: *zounds!* I'll entreat no more: "
at which exclamation Gloucester, standing between two clergymen, with a prayer-book in his hand, and affecting to be shocked, observes,

   " Oh! *do not swear*, my Lord of Buckingham,"
a line omitted in the folio of 1623, in all probability, because the

Master of the Revels, like Richard, considered "zounds" an oath, and therefore struck it out of the playhouse manuscript, from which the folio edition of "Richard III." was printed. That Shakespeare wrote it as it stands in the quarto, 1597, and in later impressions in the same form, we cannot doubt.

Page 42, line 13. Then, how to get my wing'd hand to *the booke.*] Meaning the *instrument* by which the grant was made, which document, at that time, was usually called a *book.* So in "Henry IV.," pt. 1, act iii., sc. 1.,

"By that time will our *book,* I think be drawn," referring to the agreement between Mortimer, Glendower, and Percy.

Page 42, line 16. While merit grew as *banefull* as the north.] For "baneful" the original has *bamefull,* by an evident misprint, which is corrected in a short list of *errata* at the end.

Page 43, line 5. Their *sewres* renewed still.] It may be doubted whether "sewres," in this line, is not an error for *sewtes,* or *suits,* but the passage being intelligible as it stands, we have not altered it.

Page 43, line 14. —— that kisse the *skyne,*] i. e., *skyen* or *skies,* as *eyen* is often used in poetry for *eyes.*

Page 50, line 2. Their *drumming* hearts panted their feare's alarms.] An epithet adopted from Shakespeare's "Lucrece," where he describes Tarquin standing over his yet sleeping victim,

"His *drumming* heart cheers up his burning eye."

Page 50, line 23. And *pash* to chaos.] In the Craven dialect, as well as in Norfolk and Suffolk, to *pash* is still used for to beat, or strike down, with violence. See "Holloway's General Provincial Dictionary."

Page 54, line 14. The fautors of deceipt, of truth the *scorne.*] We have not scrupled here, in accordance both with the sense and the rhime, to substitute "scorne" for *storme,* as it stands in the old copy. "Fautors" are, of course, *favourers.*

Page 61, line 4. Not those which were devoured quick to hell.] This phrase may be explained by stating that of old, especially in the old miracle-plays, hell was represented by an enormous mouth, breathing out fire and smoke: hence those supposed to be condemned to eternal torments might properly be said to be "*devoured quick to hell.*"

Page 63, line 24. —————— despaire *denaies* me.] It was not un-common to employ the verb *to denay* for to deny. Shakespeare has an instance of the kind in " Henry VI.," pt. 2, act i., sc. 3. edit. Whittaker and Co., v. 125.

Page 64, line 9. O, how I *band* the Welch.] To "ban" is to *curse*, and it is so often used in this sense, that a note seems hardly necessary.

Page 64, line 24. And set my life and kingdome on this mayne.] We have before had "mayne" employed in reference to *dice*. The corresponding passage in Shakespeare's " Richard III.," act v., sc 4, will occur to everybody.

Page 66, line 31. I started from my trance with ragefull teene,

Taking a dragon's spirit, a tyger's spleene.]

In " Richard III.," act v., sc. 3, we have,

" Inspire us with the spleen of fiery dragons."

The distress of the rhime has forced the author of " The Ghost of Richard III." into an unusual employment of the word " teen," which, in Shakespeare and other authors of the time, is ordinarily used for *sorrow*, or *grief*. See Shakespeare, edit. Whittaker and Co., i. 14, v. 441 ; vi. 388; viii. 397, 551.

Page 67, line 26. Enforce the *vildness* of mine enemie.] "Vild-ness" is a corrupt form of *vileness*, often used by old writers, and which some modern editors would strangely revive, as if correct spell-ing were to be observed in all other words, and this alone, for no assigned or assignable reason, excepted. *Vild* for *vile* is an evident blunder etymologically, as well as in every other mode of looking at the word, and it has sometimes led to the farther error of substituting *wild* for *vile*. In " Love's Labours Lost," there is a curious instance of a corruption in modern editions (pointed out in edit. Whittaker and Co., vol. ii. p. 303), where the Princess, standing in the open air, says to the king, " The roof of this court is too high to be yours, and welcome to the *wide* fields too base to be mine." Here modern editors have inserted *wild* for " wide," but they have not even the excuse that in the old copies it stands *vild*, for *all of them* have " wide." In Knight's " Pictorial Shakespeare," the corrupt text is followed—" and welcome to the *wild* fields ; " but the edit. pub-lished by Whittaker and Co., coming out soon afterwards, where the

blunder was pointed out, it was corrected, both in Mr. Knight's
" Library edition" and in his " Cabinet edition," but without
any mention of the probable means by which the error had been
detected. Perhaps this was unnecessary, and it seems to have been so
considered in other instances.

Page 68, line 22. *A pointed* comet.] In the old copy " a pointed "
is coupled, *apointed,* but it is clearly a misprint.

Page 68, line 29. My winged horse did *pegase* my desire.] This
bold manufacture of a verb out of the substantive Pegasus is, we ap-
prehend, without precedent.

Page 69, line 2. My soldiers' steele rebated.] i. e., blunted—a
very common word in this sense in Shakespeare and his contempo-
raries: in " Measure for Measure," act i., sc. 5, we have, " Doth
rebate and *blunt* his natural edge :" in " Hamlet," act iv., sc. 7, we
meet with " unbated" for *unrebated*; and in "Love's Labours
Lost," act i., sc. 1, we have " bate " for *rebate.*

Page 69, line 24. And thus performed *my* bloodie tragedie.] In
the old copy " my " is misprinted *thy.*

THE END.

LONDON:

F. SHOBERL, JUN., 51, RUPERT STREET, HAYMARKET,
PRINTER TO H. R. H. PRINCE ALBERT.

Breinigsville, PA USA
06 March 2011
257011BV00003B/268/A